A NEW OWNER'S
GUIDE TO
AMERICAN PIT BULL TERRIERS

JG-113

Overleaf: A cute APBT puppy becomes an impressive-looking adult.

Opposite page: American Pit Bull Terrier owned by Joe Rice.

The Publisher wishes to acknowledge the following owners of the dogs in this book: Gary Brewer, Traci Caggiano, Silvio Espinosa, Jr., Todd Fenstermacher, Ramona Guerrera, Leri Hanson, F. Herzig, Beth Jones, Gary McCurdy, B. Ockhuizen, Pamela Perdue, Pet Barbers, Joe Rice, J. Spronck, M. van Slijpe.

Photographers: Mary Bloom, Gary Brewer, Traci Caggiano, Wil de Veer, Lydia Fenstermacher, Isabelle Francais, Gillian Lisle, Diane Jessup, Robert Pearcy, Zuni M. Saccher.

The author acknowledges the contribution of Judy Iby of the following chapters: Sport of Purebred Dogs, Identification and Finding the Lost Dog, Traveling with Your Dog, Health Care, Behavior and Canine Communication.

© **1996 by T.F.H. Publications, Inc.**

Distributed in the UNITED STATES to the Pet Trade by T.F.H. Publications, Inc., One T.F.H. Plaza, Neptune City, NJ 07753; distributed in the UNITED STATES to the Bookstore and Library Trade by National Book Network, Inc. 4720 Boston Way, Lanham MD 20706; in CANADA to the Pet Trade by H & L Pet Supplies Inc., 27 Kingston Crescent, Kitchener, Ontario N2B 2T6; Rolf C. Hagen Inc., 3225 Sartelon St. Laurent-Montreal Quebec H4R 1E8; in CANADA to the Book Trade by Vanwell Publishing Ltd., 1 Northrup Crescent, St. Catharines, Ontario L2M 6P5 ; in ENGLAND by T.F.H. Publications, PO Box 15, Waterlooville PO7 6BQ; in AUSTRALIA AND THE SOUTH PACIFIC by T.F.H. (Australia), Pty. Ltd., Box 149, Brookvale 2100 N.S.W., Australia; in NEW ZEALAND by Brooklands Aquarium Ltd. 5 McGiven Drive, New Plymouth, RD1 New Zealand; in Japan by T.F.H. Publications, Japan—Jiro Tsuda, 10-12-3 Ohjidai, Sakura, Chiba 285, Japan; in SOUTH AFRICA by Lopis (Pty) Ltd., P.O. Box 39127, Booysens, 2016, Johannesburg, South Africa. Published by T.F.H. Publications, Inc.

MANUFACTURED IN THE
UNITED STATES OF AMERICA
BY T.F.H. PUBLICATIONS, INC.

A New Owner's Guide to
AMERICAN PIT BULL TERRIERS

Todd Fenstermacher

Contents

1996 Edition

Versatile APBTs excel at everything from conformation showing to therapy work.

Will somebody come and play with me?

An APBT models his weight pull harness.

A water bowl has many uses—this ABPT cools down on a hot day.

An adorable trio of APBT puppies.

HISTORY of the American Pit Bull Terrier

To find the origin of the American Pit Bull Terrier (APBT), you have to go back to the days of bullbaiting. Writings that date back as far as the late 1100s speak of contests where bulls and bears were "baited" by dogs. A bullbaiting consisted of a bull tied to a stake with a heavy collar and a rope. One or more dogs would be released on the bull. The dogs would try to catch the bull by the nose and hang on. If a dog was not quick, he would get caught by the bull's horns on the way in and be gouged or thrown through the air. If the dog made it to the bull's nose and got a hold, he could still be tossed off and be sent sailing through the air. If the horns did not do the dog in, then the fall could. The handlers would do their best to break the fall of the dog. Some would try to catch the dog, and some women would try to use their large aprons to soften the dog's fall. I have even seen an illustration showing poles used to break the fall of the dog. The idea of this was to get the pole under the dog so he would roll or slide down it instead of just dropping straight to the ground. Sand was often put around the baiting ring to make the landing softer as well. Keep in mind, reports showed that these dogs were often thrown as much as 30 or even 50 feet in the air.

Needless to say, a great many dogs lost their lives or were maimed. The object of the "sport" was to get the dog to pin the bull. This usually took many attempts, so breeders bred for dogs that would keep going back at the bull, no matter how many times he was thrown or how badly he was injured. This trait is what we today call *gameness*. A game dog in this case is one that will continue the battle until death. There are many stories of

Sports like bullbaiting and dog fighting required the APBT to be both quick and agile.

Dogs used for bullbaiting had to have impressive jaw strength to get a good, firm hold on the bull's nose.

these early bulldogs going back at the bull with broken legs, stomachs ripped open, and even one story about a breeder who cut the feet off his dog to show she was game enough to still bait the bull on stumps.

These early bulldogs were also baited with everything from bears to lions, though these were not animals normally owned by the common man. The commoner would bait his dog against other animals such as badgers, occasionally monkeys, and other dogs. This takes us to the very first of the breed we now know as the American Pit Bull Terrier.

There are two schools of thought on what breed(s) made up the foundation of the modern APBT. Some say it is simply the original bulldog bred for the purpose of dog fighting. Some of the artwork depicting bullbaiting does show dogs that look similar to the modern APBT. It is hard to come to any concrete conclusions from this because much of the artwork varied in how the dogs were depicted. Some artwork shows the dogs as being short, squat dogs with short, undershot muzzles, and some artwork portrayed the bullbaiting dogs as looking much like the APBT. The more popular theory is that the early pit dogs were bulldog and terrier crosses. The terrier believed to be used is the now-extinct English White Terrier. The idea

The American Pit Bull Terrier eventually resulted from bulldog and terrier crosses—this combination produced a dog with speed, agility, and gameness.

behind this theory was that the terrier added the speed and agility and the bulldog added the gameness. Even the name American Pit Bull Terrier suggests this is the case. At this time, the bulldog and terrier crosses were already being used in ratting contests. In such a contest the dog would be timed to see how fast he could kill a designated number of rats. Either way, the APBT is a descendant of these dogs used in the early dog-on-dog matches. I think that is something we all can agree on!

Dog fighting became quite popular in both England and Ireland. It was a sport the common man could afford to participate in. This sport eliminated the need for bulls, bears, and a space large enough for a baiting. This brought a "dog sport" into the reach of the common man. The outlawing of the sport of bullbaiting in 1835 only sparked even greater interest in the sport of dog fighting.

Before the time of the Civil War, these fighting dogs and their sport made their way to the United States and the breed quickly gained popularity. In 1898, Mr. C. B. Bennett formed the United Kennel Club. This was the first registry for the breed now called the American Pit Bull Terrier (APBT). The United Kennel Club (UKC) published a standard as well as rules for pit contests. The UKC still exists today and now registers many other breeds as well as the APBT. In 1909, Guy McCord started the American Dog Breeders' Association to register the APBT. The ADBA is today the favored registry of the American Pit Bull Terrier fancier. The ADBA sanctions conformation shows as well as weight pull events.

Do you remember Pete, the APBT from the Little Rascals *TV series? If so, you can probably see some resemblance in Thumbelina!*

The American Kennel Club (AKC) recognized the breed in 1936. There was some debate over what the name would be, though. Yankee Terrier was one popular choice, but they stuck with American Staffordshire Terrier. They dropped the word "pit" (how politically correct!) but the mention of Staffordshire is a throwback to the days of pit matches in England.

The AKC chose "Pete" of the *Hal Roach's Little Rascals* fame to be the first APBT registered as an American Staffordshire Terrier. Actually, the dog chosen was only one of the American Pit Bull Terriers used in that series. If you look at the series, you will see that there were actually several American Pit Bull Terriers used as Pete. There was an APBT in the series before Pete named Pal that was supposed to be Pete's father (at least in the series).

The APBT was featured as Buster Brown's dog Tighe. Theodore Roosevelt brought his APBT to the White House. In 1914 an APBT was even given the honor of representing the

United States in a World War I poster. "I'm neutral, but not afraid of any of them" is the caption under the dog. A very good example of APBT attitude! I have seen a photo of Charlie Chaplin out walking with an APBT. Helen Keller owned an APBT, as did Fred Astaire and General George Patton. On the cover of the album *The Quintessential Billie Holiday* (Volume 3, 1936–1937), Ms. Holiday is shown holding an APBT. Today, the APBT is portrayed in music videos and on the covers of CDs as being anything but the friendly dog that the APBT actually is.

Many of the American Pit Bull Terrier fanciers weren't looking for AKC recognition. Many good working breeds have suffered from people breeding for show ring competition and many APBT fanciers were afraid of this happening. This, combined with how the AKC often tried to distance the pit fighting history from the breed, did not sit well with some fanciers. The UKC began to dual-register American Pit Bull Terriers and American Staffordshire Terriers as the same breed. Even though there would be a designation for each breed in the pedigree, you could still dual-register these "crosses."

For instance, take the

In the early days of pit fighting, the Staffordshire Bull Terrier and the APBT were thought of as much the same dog. Today, the two are recognized as separate breeds.

This friendly dog is a fine example of one of the APBT's most important roles–that of the playful and loyal family pet!

Staffordshire Bull Terrier. This separate breed started out as simply being the preferred pit dog strain used in Staffordshire in the early pit fighting days in England. This separate strain bred true-to-type and was recognized in 1935 by the English Kennel Club as its own breed. Today, no one would consider a Staffordshire Bull Terrier to be an APBT even though at one time they were thought of as the same breed. In this way, history is repeating itself again with the APBT and the American Staffordshire, as they are becoming (or have become) two separate breeds. By now, few people with game-bred APBTs would consider crossing their dogs with American Staffordshires any more than an American Staffordshire breeder would want to breed to APBTs. Still, you will find those with American Staffordshires that want the name American Pit Bull Terrier for their dogs just the same.

Illegal pit matches have been going on since the early days of the formation of this breed, but these matches were not as "underground" as they are today. In 1976, a federal law was passed against dog fighting. Before this, dog fighting was a only a misdemeanor, where now it is a felony in almost every state in America. This is not to say that the matches don't still go on,

because they do. Those involved are doing so at great personal risk. While most people condemn dog fighting, it is ironic how many of the same people are devout fans of the very animal that dog fighting has produced—the American Pit Bull Terrier!

No other aspect of the history of this breed is more important than the American Pit Bull Terrier's role as a trusted family pet. The stories of zany antics, extreme loyalty, and unquestioned bravery go back to the beginning of the breed. Those of us who know and love the breed know it as companion, guardian, playmate, clown, confidant, and just plain the best dog out there. They make one heck of a good bed warmer to boot!

With today's exploding popularity of the breed there have come breeders who know little and care even less about what a true APBT really is. These people are crossing the APBT with whatever is available, breeding for human aggression, and producing some unstable dogs. They sell these dogs cheap and without registration papers. The pity is that they call these dogs "pit bulls"and many think this is the same dog as the APBT. The best illustration of this is the fact that the APBT has been in this country for so many years but few knew what an APBT was until the early 1980s. The APBT has been used as a family pet, pit fighter, and catch dog for a long time but you never read about "pit bull" attacks until recent years. If the APBTs were really the vicious, unstable dogs that the media portrays them as, then where were all the stories about attacks before? Why didn't Helen Keller get attacked by her APBT? How did Theodore Roosevelt keep an APBT in the White House without someone getting bitten? Back then, there wasn't the problem of uneducated people breeding unstable dogs and calling them "pit bulls."

It is important that stable, even-tempered APBTs continue to be bred so that people will have a positive impression of the breed.

Author Todd Fenstermacher and one of his affectionate APBT friends. APBTs love being petted and getting attention.

CHARACTER of the APBT

An American Pit Bull Terrier is a fantastic choice for a family pet for anyone who fully understands the breed and its unique characteristics. The breed is very submissive, intelligent, and eager to please, which makes it quite easy to train. These dogs excel at everything from advanced Schutzhund work to complicated pet tricks. Simple everyday commands are a snap to train them to do. The APBT is a very stable dog with a solid temperament. The last figures I saw from the American Canine Temperament Testing Association showed the APBT ranking fourth in the list of breeds with the highest percentages of passing. A total of 95% of the APBTs tested passed, which is really saying something about the breed since the average for all breeds combined was only 77% passing.

The APBT also makes a great choice for a pet in a home with children. They are gentle with and very tolerant of the little ones. One of the results of the years of breeding for pit fighting is that these dogs have incredible pain tolerance. They think nothing of having their ears pulled or being plopped on by children. The APBT seems to thrive on the borderline abusive treatment children can dish out. The only thing to watch out for is that tail! A happy APBT can beat you silly with his whip-like tail.

Due to the nature of what the APBT was bred for, it is important to socialize him early. Take him to where there are other dogs and discourage any signs of aggression. Do this and you should have a very friendly dog that loves to meet other animals. Let him see how happy it makes you to see him playing friendly and it should become a part of his personality. Of course, as in any breed, there will still be some dog-aggressive APBTs that will remain that way even with

APBTs are great with children! This APBT was happy to pose for a picture with a few of his playmates.

Although the APBT is not naturally aggressive toward humans, the presence of an APBT in your home will probably make an intruder think twice about choosing it for a target.

thorough socialization. Still, even some APBTs that have been used in dog fighting have been known to be friendly with other same-sex dogs, as long as the other dog doesn't show any signs of aggression. I have seen this firsthand.

Another positive attribute is that the APBT makes for a very serious deterrent to crime. Nothing will keep a burglar on the outside of your window like seeing the big head of an APBT on the inside. The APBT really doesn't make for a good choice as a guard dog, though. It is the APBT's nature to be a very trusting and social dog with people, including strangers. The APBT is a dog that normally doesn't bark much either, although there are some exceptions. For this reason the APBT doesn't even make a good "alarm dog." There are many breeds that make fantastic guard dogs, but the APBT isn't one of them. Of course the APBT can be trained for this type of duty, but it takes a lot of professional training to get one to go against his nature and bite a person, because for countless generations "man biters" were culled right on the spot. Dog fighters would see a "man biter" as being a weak dog, one that was less than game. It was viewed as a sign of fear in the dog. Along with this, an APBT that could not be trusted *not* to bite a person could not be used in a pit match.

A very attractive point about this breed is that they are relatively low-maintenance. They have short coats that need very little grooming of any kind. If you hit enough sidewalks on your walks with the dogs, they won't need their nails clipped much at all. Bathe them when they get dirty, keep the tartar off their teeth, and keep up on the shots and heartworm medicine—that is about all. They do thrive on physical activity, so get out and get some fresh air with your dog. Go for a walk or a jog, or let him pull you around on your rollerblades. You will be doing both of you some good.

Another plus is that the APBT is not a dog that is naturally man-aggressive. This goes against most of what you read in the paper or hear in the news about the breed, but it is the truth. Many APBTs have been stolen by people who just walk up and take them without a struggle. I know several APBT kennels that actually keep other breeds of dogs to guard the APBTs from being stolen. When you think about it, the pit fighter could not have been a man-aggressive dog. In the pit, the dog was often handled by a man other than the dog's owner, and there was another handler in the pit along with a referee. If the APBT were an aggressive dog, these other men wouldn't be safe in such a small, enclosed area with two dogs doing battle. The countless generations of breeding for combat dogs that would not be man-aggressive have bred that tendency out of the APBT. It wasn't until recent years, when the APBT became so popular, that some uninformed, careless individuals actually

Since APBTs were bred to be submissive to man, the truth is that they are not naturally man-aggressive—unless mishandled or carelessly trained.

started to breed *for* man-aggressive dogs.

The role of the APBT today is more as family pet than anything else. A small percentage of the owners still use them for their original purpose as the pound-for-pound best fighting dog in history. They still excel at this and most would agree that the "game-bred" APBTs of today are better pit fighters than the ones of the past. The qualities the APBT has picked up from being bred for the pit have made it an outstanding dog for a variety of other purposes.

Through his breeding and background, the APBT has acquired a multitude of qualities which make him a versatile and functional dog.

Hunting is one example. APBTs are often used for wild boar hunting. There are even some "hog dog rodeos" where APBTs make a fine showing as catch dogs. These contests are far less brutal than the actual hunts these dogs go on. The "rodeos" are timed contests where the dog has to catch a hog, handlers flip the hog, then take the dog off the hog with a breaking stick. The winner is the one that can do this the quickest. There is a big effort right now to outlaw these contests.

Exercise is as important for dogs as it is for humans! Bonehead likes to go for walks to the local shops to check out what's going on.

The role of the catch dog on the hunt

is to get a hold on the side of the boar's head and hold it so the hunter can flip it, tie it, stab it, or shoot it. The boars are incredibly fast for weighing up to 300 pounds. The speed and agility of these huge boars is amazing. The catch dog has to get in to get his hold without the boar catching him first. The boar can easily kill the dog with his tusks by slashing, goring, or tossing the dog through the air. When, and if, the dog gets a hold without getting caught, there is the problem of holding the boar. The APBT will have to twist and contort to avoid the boar's tusks as the boar shakes his head from side to side trying to get the dog off of him. If the tusks don't get the dog, he could still end up under the boar's hooves, which are sharper than you may think. The dog could be killed in the blink of an eye either way.

Although not commonly thought of as a show dog, many APBTs participate in conformation showing. They are truly impressive-looking dogs.

For this reason, the catch dogs are usually not released until the hunters are in place to end the battle quickly. Most hunters use a pack of bay dogs to keep the boar in place until the catch dog can be walked up on a leash. Some hunters will instead use air boats and chase down the boars. The air boats allow the hunters to safely get both themselves and the dog close to the boar before releasing the dog. The hunters have to have the utmost faith in their dog's ability to maintain their hold. If the dog lets go, the boar can turn on the hunter, who at that time may be right in harm's way. This sport tests the dog's courage and also to some degree his gameness. On top of this, the dog must be a quick learner. There is little room for mistakes and few dogs get a second chance to get it right.

Today, the APBT is often a conformation show dog. Even though the breed isn't commonly known as a "show dog," the APBT shows have great turnouts. Few can argue that these dogs are not something to look at. It's always fun to go out and show off your dog and admire the other APBTs. I encourage people to go out to the shows, to support the local club hosting the show by entering their dogs, and to just have fun with it. The APBT clubs could use the support. They do more than just host shows; they try to promote a positive image of the breed and often have rescue programs. A rescue group takes in dogs that have no homes and may otherwise be

euthanized in shelters. Plus, you can find a lot of hard-to-get items especially made for APBTs at these shows.

Along with the conformation judging at these shows, there are often weight pull events. This is where the APBT, fitted with a special weight pull harness, is connected to a sled or cart and has to pull a designated weight 15 feet in under 60 seconds. First the dogs are weighed to place them in their respective weight classes. Then each dog pulls the cart with the starting weight. The weight is increased after all the dogs have pulled. They all pull again, the weight is increased again, etc. If the dog can't pull the weight the required distance in 60 seconds, he is credited with the last weight he was able to pull. When no dogs are left, the judges tally up which dogs won for each class. They also give awards for the most weight pulled and the most weight pulled per pound (weight of the dog). By the end, not only are raw strength and endurance tested, but also to some degree the "never give up" attitude associated with gameness.

Describing the personality of the APBT is no easy task. "Entertaining clown" would best sum up one of the popular aspects of the dogs. The more of your attention they get, the sillier they can act. You may see an APBT tear off in a running fit around the yard, jump through the air, flop on the ground, and turn around to make sure you are still watching before he does it all again.

The submissive nature of this breed can be attributed to its being bred for pit fighting. An APBT that would challenge its owner was commonly put down on the spot, obviously eliminating dogs with this trait from the breeding program. This works well with training. When scolded, the APBT will

This APBT is competing in a weight-pull event. The APBT's power and strength make him a natural for this type of competition.

20

get a very sorry and hurt look about him. There is no need to make physical corrections with a dog like this.

Most people are surprised to find out just how quiet and affectionate these dogs really are. The stereotype is that these dogs are vicious, loud animals that want to eat strangers. Nothing could be further from this breed's true nature. Granted, I have seen APBTs that have been "trained" to be like this. I use the word "trained" very loosely, the word "abused" is more like it. The fact is, you are far more likely to be licked, pawed, and cuddled by an APBT. Don't be surprised if you don't hear an APBT bark, either. The last APBT kennel I

APBTs seem to be fascinated by their water bowls, often using them to play with or chew on. This APBT was a little more creative in finding a use for his bowl!

visited had over 20 dogs and only two of the bunch ever made a sound. The rest were straining to get close enough to have me pet them, as any typical APBT would.

One thing you will notice about the APBT is that they love physical work! When you consider what their original purpose was, though, it makes perfect sense. An APBT getting ready for a match had to do miles on top of miles of walking and running, just for starters. Good luck trying to walk your APBT to exhaustion! If not trained to heel, an APBT will want to lead the way on walks, pulling for as long as he can. It is also common for dogs chained outside to find ways to exercise themselves. Probably the most common way is playing with/ eating their water bowls, and I know of some that will hang from trees if chained out close enough to grab a branch. Keep in mind that the APBT has to support not only his total body weight, but also the weight of a heavy chain.

One of the most impressive things about an APBT's personality is sheer bravery. They can often get themselves in trouble with this one! An APBT seems to see himself as indestructible and will try anything once, twice if he survives the first attempt! I remember once walking at an APBT kennel looking at dogs. Suddenly, there were a couple of puppies at my feet. I had just seen these pups in a 6-foot high chain-link kennel run with a latch too high for them to open. When the breeder and I went to investigate, we found the remaining litter actually climbing the fence and leaping off the top to get out. They figured out that they could put their paws in the fence and "walk" up it. Once they figured this out, they had to be kept in kennels with tops on them.

Speaking of APBTs getting themselves in trouble, one of their traits, if they are not socialized, is dog aggression. Mostly this is just a same-sex problem (male on male, or female on female). The best cure for this is early socialization. Show your new pet that dog aggression is not going to be stood for. Still, you need to keep in mind that if another dog presses the issue and tries to start something with an APBT...well, let's just say it is not in their nature to "turn the other cheek." A well-socialized APBT should not go looking for a fight at all. He should instead be friendly and playful even with other same-sex dogs. Just watch for another dog trying to dominate your APBT. Be responsible! Do not ever let your APBT get into this

The APBT is very gentle around children and makes a good pet for a family with children. Here, Mako is spending some time with his friend Cody.

situation. Socialize and stay away from aggressive dogs and you will be fine.

You may be surprised to find out just how gentle the APBT really is. Sure, they will not back down from a fight, but if the fight is not taken to them, they are as gentle a pet as you could want—especially with children and smaller animals. Between the APBT's very high pain tolerance and very protective, gentle demeanor toward children, I do not think I could come up with a better breed choice for the family pet. Many APBTs are kept in homes with cats, other dogs, birds, etc., and there is no trouble at all. My cat often curls up with my APBTs to sleep. When they play, the cat is the one who is the most aggressive! The APBTs simply paw at her a little and may touch up against her with an open mouth, but never bite her.

The APBT is known for his muscularity and overall strength, particularly his jaw strength.

The special abilities that set the American Pit Bull Terrier apart from other breeds can all be traced back to their original purpose, dog fighting. The APBT exhibits an incredibly high pain tolerance which, of course, would be needed in dog fighting. The dog matches were set up to make the other dog quit, not to kill the opponent. If the APBT could not take a good amount of punishment, then he would quit and lose the match. He could quit by either trying to jump over the pit wall (only 32-36 inches tall) or by failing to "scratch" (failing to go across the pit and restart the fight after being separated).

Pit fighting also bred high endurance in the APBT. The fighting dog had to be ready to go for as long as the match lasted...and that could be hours! The longest reported pit match was over five hours long! That is why the APBT thrives on physical work, much like a Greyhound loves to run or a retriever loves the hunt. It is something that the breed has been bred to love.

The sheer strength of the APBT is legendary, both jaw strength and overall body strength. It is plain to see why jaw strength would be so important. A hard biting dog can have his opponent looking for a way out of the fight in order to avoid further punishment. The overall physical strength would be needed to wrestle the opponent onto his back or into a corner where a better hold could be achieved. All this breeding for physical strength has resulted in the APBT today being one of the best pound-for-pound weight pull dogs. Both the overall physical strength, and jaw strength in particular, has made for one top-notch catch dog.

The most important trait gained by pit fighting is gameness. Gameness is the APBT's drive to keep going, no matter what. It is the one trait that most sets the APBT apart from other dogs. There are other dogs that have fighting pasts and may have actually retained some level of gameness, but not to the level of the APBT. It is the "do or die trying" attitude of the APBT that is the most impressive. Do not confuse gameness with dog aggression; they are quite different. Any dog can pick a fight (be dog-aggressive) but a game dog will see the fight through to the end no matter what the outcome.

Although the APBT is a great family pet, it is not a breed for everyone. Only very responsible pet owners should consider this dog. Keeping and caring for an APBT is very different from owning other breeds. First you have to understand the dog's attitude. The APBT is loving and gentle, but also very protective and will not turn his back on a fight. You need to know when a situation is going to get you in trouble with your APBT and avoid it. An APBT defending himself or protecting you will most likely be seen as being vicious and aggressive by people who only know the breed by what they read in the paper. I know that is not fair and not right, but it is reality!

People looking to own an APBT need to be willing to educate themselves. They need to be the kind of people who will listen to the advice of the breeder and other owners of APBTs. Their firsthand knowledge is invaluable to the first-time owner.

A person getting an APBT should not be someone with a big ego where the dog is concerned. Many macho types own this breed and are giving APBTs a bad name for all of us. Sure, you may well have the toughest dog on the block, but that is the *last* reason to own one of these dogs. Owning an APBT does not make you a "tough guy" so do not fool yourself. If this is one of the reasons you are considering this breed then you need more help than any dog is going to provide!

An APBT owner needs to be someone who is going to take the time to train and socialize his dog. A well-trained and socialized APBT is a joy to have around the home, as well as the neighborhood. Often, people who don't have firsthand knowledge of this breed believe all the negative press. They may not like seeing an APBT around the neighborhood. This is where the APBT owner has to be patient and take the time to try to educate these people about what kind of dog the APBT really is. It may not be easy, but it is well worth it. The right kind of APBT owner knows this. He knows that we can only change the negative image one person, one block, and one neighborhood at a time.

Lastly, the ideal owner of the APBT is someone who is loyal to his dog and the breed. He knows that owning a dog is a lifetime commitment. He does what he can to make life good for the APBT in his home as well as outside it by promoting a positive image of his dog, and therefore, of the breed. If we don't all take an active part in doing this, we may actually see a ban on the breed in our lifetime. It has already happened in parts of Europe and there are people proposing it in the United States as well.

An APBT owner needs to make a commitment to properly training and socializing his dog, and therefore to promoting a positive image of the breed.

CONFORMATION of the APBT

Look first at the overall profile of the dog. Ideally, he should be "square" when viewed from the side. That is, about as long from the shoulder to the point of his hip as he is tall from the top of the shoulder to the ground. Such a dog will stand high and have maximum leverage for his weight. This means that standing normally with the hock slightly back of the hip, the dog's base (where his feet are) will be slightly longer than his height. Using the hip and shoulder as guides will keep the viewer from being fooled by the way the dog is standing.

Overall, the APBT should be a well-muscled dog with a profile that is "square" in appearance.

Height to weight ratio is critical. Since dogs are fought at nearly identical weights, the bigger the dog you have at the weights, the better your chances. Hence, stocky dogs with long bodies, heavy shoulders and thick legs usually lose to taller, rangier opponents.

Nature usually blesses a tall rangy dog with a fairly long neck which is a tremendous advantage in that it enables him to reach a stifle when his opponent may have his front leg, to take an ear to hold off a shorter necked opponent, or to reach the chest himself when the other dog is trying to hold him off. The neck should be heavily muscled right up to the base of the skull.

Secondly, look at his back end. That's the drive train of any four legged animal. A Bulldog does 80% of his work off his hips and back legs.

A long sloping hip is most important. By its very

Poison is an example of a more rangy APBT—notice her long, muscular neck.

length, it gives leverage to the femur or thigh bone. A long hip will give the dog a slightly roached backed appearance. Hence the "low set" tail so often spoken of.

The hip should be broad. A broad hip will carry with it a broad loin and permits a large surface for the attachment of the gluteal and the *biceps femoris* muscles, the biggest drivers in the power train.

The femur or thigh bone should be shorter than the tibia or lower leg bone. This means that the stifle joint will be in the upper one third of the hind leg. It is not uncommon to see dogs with a low stifle. They are usually impressively muscled because of the bigger biceps femoris, but are surprisingly weak and slow on the back legs because of leverage lost by the long thigh. A short femur and long tibia usually mean a well bent stifle, which in turn leads to a well bent hock. This last is really a critical aspect of wrestling ability. When a dog finds himself being driven backward, he must rely on natural

The musculature and structure of the APBT's hips and back legs are very important, as they comprise the "drive train" that powers the dog's movement.

The APBT must have a deep rib cage to house his large lungs. This dog also has the breed's characteristic low-set tail.

springiness of the well bent hock and stifle to control his movement. Dogs with straight or the frequently seen double jointed hock of many of the Dibo bred dogs will wrestle well as long as muscle power can sustain them, but if pushed, will tire in the back end more quickly and soon lose their wrestling ability.

Thirdly, look at the front end. He should have a deep rib cage, well sprung at the top, but tapering to the bottom. Deep and elliptical, almost narrow is preferred to the round and barrel chested. The rib cage houses the lungs which are not storage tanks, but pumps. The ribs are like a bellows. Their efficiency is related to the difference in volume between contraction and expansion. A barrel chested dog, in addition to carrying more weight for his height, has an air pump with a short stroke. He must take more breaths to get the same volume of air. Depth of rib cage gives more room for large lungs.

Shoulders should be a little wider than the rib cage at the

eighth rib. Too narrow a shoulder does not support adequate musculature but too wide a shoulder makes a dog slow and adds unnecessary weight. The scapula (shoulder blade) should be at a 45 degree or less slope to the ground and broad and flat. The humerus should be at an equal angle in the opposite direction and long enough that the elbow comes below the bottom of the rib cage. The elbows should lie flat, the humerus running almost parallel to the spine, not out at elbows which gives a wide "English Bulldog" stance. This type of shoulder is more easily dislocated or broken.

The forearm should be only slightly longer than the humerus and heavy and solid—nearly twice the thickness of the metatarsal bones at the hock. The front legs and shoulders must be capable of sustaining tremendous punishment and heaviness can be an asset here.

The relationship between front legs and back should be, at first appearance, of a heavy front and a delicate back. This is because in an athletic dog, the metatarsal bones, hock and lower part of the tibia will be light, fine and springy. The front legs will be heavy and solid looking. The experienced Bulldog man, however, will note the wide hip, loin and

Although head size varies in today's APBTs, the head should always be in proportion with the rest of the body, about two-thirds the width of the shoulders.

powerful thigh which make the back end the most muscular. The head varies more in the present day Pit Bull than any other part of the body, probably because its conformation has the least to do with whether he wins or loses. However, there are certain attributes which appear to be of advantage. First, its overall size. Too big a head simply carries more weight and increases the chances of having to fight a bigger dog. Too small a head is easily punished by a nose fighter and is especially easy for an ear fighter to shake. In an otherwise well proportioned dog, the head will appear to be about two thirds the width of the shoulders and about 25% wider at the cheeks than the neck at the base of the skull. Back of the head to the stop should be about the same distance as from the stop to the tip of the nose. The bridge of the nose should be well developed, which will make the area directly under the eyes considerably wider than the head at the base of the ears. Depth from the top of the head to the bottom of the jaw is important. The jaw is closed by the temporal fossa muscle exerting

The structure of the head, jaw, and teeth combine to give the APBT incredible jaw strength and biting power.

pressure on the coronoid process. The deeper the head at this point, (that is, between the zygomatic arch and the angular process of the bottom of the jaw) the more likely the dog is to have leverage advantage both in closing the jaw and in keeping it closed. A straight, box-like muzzle and well-developed mandible will not have much to do with biting power but will endure more punishment. "Lippy" dogs are continually fanging themselves in a fight, which works greatly to their disadvantage. Teeth should meet in the front, but more importantly, the canines or fangs should slip tightly together, the upper behind the lower when the mouth is closed. The eye is elliptical when viewed from the front.

In general, such a head will be wedge-shaped when viewed either from the top or side, round when viewed from the front. Skin should be thick and loose, but not in folds. It should appear to fit the dog tightly except around the neck and chest. Here the skin should be loose enough to show vertical folds even in a well conditioned dog.

The set of the tail is most important. It should be low. The length should come just above the point of the hock, thick at the base and tapering to a point at the end and should hang down like a pump handle when relaxed.

The feet should be small and set high on the pasterns. The gait of the dog should be light and springy.

Most of the above relates to skeletal features of the dog. When we look at muscles, from the breeder's standpoint, it is much more important to look at the genetic features of musculature than those features due to conditioning. A genetically powerful dog can be a winner in the hands of an even inept trainer, but a genetically weak dog needs a good matchmaker to win. Conditioning won't do much for him.

Unlike many other breeds, any coat color or color combination is acceptable for the APBT. Here is a handsome example of a brindle coat.

Think of bones as levers with the joints as the fulcrum and the muscles being the power source. The power being applied to the lever is more effective the farther away from the fulcrum it is applied. Muscles should be long, with attachments deep down the bone, well past the joint. Short muscled dogs are impressive looking but not athletic. A muscle's power value lies in its ability to contract. The greater the difference between its relaxed state and its contracted state, the greater the power.

The coat of the dog can be any color or any combination of colors. It should be short and bristled. The gloss of the coat usually reflects the health of the dog and is important to an athletic Pit Bulldog.

Above all, the American Pit Bull Terrier is an all-around athlete. His body is called on for speed, power, agility and

Sinbad's coat is an example of "blue merle" coloration, which is very rare in the APBT.

stamina. He must be balanced in all directions. Too much of one thing robs him of another. He is not a model formed according to human specialists. In his winning form he is a fighting machine—a thing of beauty.

In judging the American Pit Bull Terrier 100 points will be possible for the ideal dog. The breakdown is as follows:

Overall Appearance	20 Points
Attitude of Dog	10 Points
Head & Neck	15 Points
Front End of Dog	20 Points
Back End of Dog	30 Points
Tail and Coat	5 Points
	Total 100 Points

SELECTING the Right APBT

Before getting an American Pit Bull Terrier of your own, you will have quite a lot to consider. Most importantly, you will want to know how to recognize a good example of the breed. First and foremost is the temperament. You can have the most beautiful dog in the world, but if he is afraid of his own shadow you may grow weary of this dog. The same holds true for overly aggressive dogs. No one wants (or should want!) a dog that shows aggression at everything that moves. Your prospect should be a friendly, outgoing dog or pup that is happy to greet you as a stranger. The prospect should neither cower nor become aggressive when he hears loud noises. A little show of avoidance is normal, but should be followed by curiosity. A good example of this is a breeder I know who was out working in the yard with a litter of pups around him. He watched the pups as he dropped a tool on the concrete slab. One of the pups ran right in at the noise, showing no sign of avoidance at all. The rest of the litter jumped at the sound but then got curious to see just what had caused the racket. The more aggressive pup went to a home where he was to be used more as a guard dog than as a house pet.

How can you pick just one? This row of adorable APBT pups makes the choice difficult!

When it comes to the overall general appearance, it will be different depending on if you are looking at an adult or a pup. If you are getting adult, you can look at the standard to understand what you are looking for. If you are getting a pup,

APBT pups have that "puppy cuteness" that make them hard to resist.

then you will want to look at the parents, if you can, and other examples of similar breeding. APBT puppies go through some very awkward stages where they seem to look like less than the best example of what you are looking for in an adult dog. For example, the ears may look huge and very "houndlike" when the pup is young, but as an adult the dog's head should fill out to fit those ears quite well.

Next you will need to determine if you would rather have a male or female American Pit Bull Terrier. Males tend to run larger than females, but also keep in mind that there is a huge variation in size in this breed. Males often resemble the standard more closely than females in other dog breeds, but the difference is not as great with the American Pit Bull Terrier. Females have been known to be a bit easier to housetrain. If you do not have a yard and will have to hand-walk your dog when it needs to go out, keep in mind that a female is much more likely to empty her bladder in one shot. Males will want to hit several different places before they are done. That may not sound like such a big deal now, but wait until it is raining or the temperature is frigid!

PUPPY VS. ADULT

You will need to decide if you want either a pup or an adult APBT. Some of the advantages of getting an adult are that you see how the dog is going to look for the rest of his life, you can see if the dog has developed any genetic problems that you might not be able to spot in a young puppy, and you will probably not have to housebreak an adult. The adult may have had other training in obedience, and the adult will be able to withstand a whole lot more roughhousing from children than a pup could. The adult will oftentimes already be spayed or neutered. You can better see in the adult if there is going to be a problem with aggression toward people or other animals. This is something you would have a much harder time spotting in a puppy.

If you're not thrilled with the idea of trying to housebreak a puppy, an adult APBT might be the better choice for you!

On the downside, the adult may have already been trained in ways you rather he wasn't. For instance, he may have been encouraged to pull when he is being walked, he may have been allowed up on the furniture, he may have been allowed to beg at the table, etc. These may be hard habits to break, though this is not to say that they can't be. Age is also something to keep in mind when considering an adult APBT. A healthy APBT will live into his early or mid-teens. I have known some that have lived to be nearly 20 years old, but that is more the exception.

One of the biggest reasons people end up with a puppy instead of an adult is that puppy appeal! There is nothing cuter! A puppy can be raised in *your* home learning *your* habits. The puppy can be taught the whole family routine and what his role is right from the beginning of his life. With a puppy, you will know just how he has been socialized and trained, and if there were any traumatic events that may bother him later in life. For example, an American Pit Bull Terrier sprayed with pepper spray by a mailman may still like all strangers...as long as they aren't wearing blue and driving in a white truck! By knowing the pup/dog's full life history you will know if there might be things like this that would trigger your dog to act fearful or aggressive.

It's easy to fall in love with a face like this, but make sure that your decision to bring a puppy home is well thought out.

As cute, cuddly, and playful as puppies can be, they are a whole lot of work! First, the puppy will have to be trained and socialized with other animals as well as with new people. Housetraining may well change your schedule around. A puppy has less control of his bowels and bladder, so he will have to be let out often. This means putting off the morning coffee until the puppy has had his trip outside. It also means getting up early on days off so the puppy can keep on a schedule of his own.

Puppies chew. For some reason puppies will often spit out the most elaborate, well-thought-out, and expensive toys just so they can gnaw on the coffee table. Close supervision will keep this to a minimum but you can expect *some* damage before this stage is passed. Many pet stores carry bitter tasting pastes you can put on areas your puppy shouldn't be chewing but for some reason seems to like.

Puppies may also have genetic traits that will not be apparent until adulthood. This may be as simple as some minor flaw preventing him from fitting the standard just right at maturity to something that could cause serious health problems later on in life. With the APBT, though, the instances of genetic disease are few and far between. Genetic flaws are so rare that some breeders do inbreed with few, if any, negative results.

FINDING A BREEDER

Now, if you know just what you are looking for in an American Pit Bull Terrier, then it is time to discuss your requirements with a breeder. In many cases a breeder will have both parents on the property and possibly even the grandparents. There will be other examples of his breeding around for you to look at. This will be the best way of seeing how you can expect your puppy to turn out. Many breeders will also offer a health guarantee on the puppy. The breeder will have the litters registered and can show you the pedigrees for the dogs.

Ask the breeder to supply references. Check with these people who have bought dogs from this breeder to see how they have been treated and how their dogs have turned out. Any breeder will talk about how great he is, but it is a lot better to hear the praise coming from past customers! Ask the

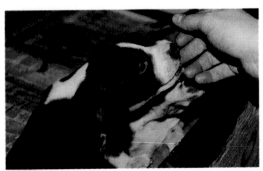

If you visit an APBT kennel, the puppies and dogs should respond well to your being there. They should approach you and welcome your petting.

breeder about the puppies' shot records and when the pups were wormed. Records of this should be readily available. If they aren't, then it is a good idea to look for your APBT elsewhere. Ask about how the prospect has been socialized. Many good dogs have been "ruined" by being isolated at the kennel all their lives. Many times you can reverse the effect, but it will take time and patience. A good breeder will know how to socialize the pups so they will not be fearful when they leave the kennel or meet new people.

Make sure that the breeder runs a quality facility and that all of the dogs are clean, healthy, and well taken care of.

While at the breeder's place be sure to make mental notes of how the dogs are kept. Are the dogs' areas clean and well-kept? Are the dogs kept in secure enclosures or on good, solid tie-out chains? Do the dogs all look healthy and well maintained? Ask if you can approach the adult dogs. How do they respond to you being there? The dogs should all be friendly and should greet you warmly, wanting you to pet them. See if the adults are what you would want your puppy to be at maturity.

The breeders may very well ask you just as many questions as you ask them. It is a good sign if they do. It shows that they are concerned about what kind of home the puppy will have. Be honest and up front with the breeders so they can direct you to a puppy that will best suit your home. You will want to develop a relationship with the breeder you choose. Breeders can be a wealth of information on the particular traits of your dog and the changes you can expect as your APBT matures, plus they can recommend veterinarians and trainers in your area. The breeder will also know of breed clubs in the area. It is good to have as many knowledgeable APBT fanciers around as possible!

The cost of the dog may be a bit higher from a breeder than, say, from someone advertising in the paper, but when you consider the benefits, especially to the first-time APBT buyer, it can be well worth it. The breeder may have different prices for "pet" and "show" quality dogs and pups. What separates the pet from the show quality APBT are simple physical traits. It may be something as simple as the color of the nose or the length of the ears. If you do not plan to show or breed your APBT then a pet quality dog is something to consider, especially if you are on a budget. The pet quality prospect will make just as good a family pet. Pet quality APBTs should not be bred. Many times the breeder will actually withhold the registration papers until you can prove you have either spayed or neutered your APBT.

Watch out for a breeder that offers you a "deal" on a puppy if you agree to breed it at maturity and give part or all of the litter back to him. It is impossible to know exactly how the puppy will be at maturity. Even the best lines will occasionally produce a dog that is less than breeding quality. A breeder offering such a "deal" may be more interested in making money than in producing the best possible APBT. If you are offered such a deal on a young puppy, it is a good idea to talk to other breeders.

Sometimes a breeder will offer an adult dog in a similar situation. Many breeders that are trying to get ahead on their breeding program but have limited space will "farm out" a few adults this way. This allows them to see

A reputable breeder should be concerned with preserving the quality of the breed and always strive to produce the best puppies possible.

If you decide that an adult dog will better fit your lifestyle, you can often find quality adult APBTs through breeders or rescue groups.

a good adult APBT get a good family home, and at the same time still be able to use that APBT in their breeding programs. The registration on such a dog may show the APBT as being co-owned by both you and the breeder. I am personally in this situation now. My female house dog is at her breeder's place about to have a litter. After the litter is weaned she will be back home with us. I don't recommend this to anyone new to the breed or to the first-time dog owner. You should only enter into such an agreement if you have gotten to know the breeder quite well. If you should get an adult APBT this way, make sure you both have an understanding of what happens if one of you moves out of the area, the dog meets with an early death, etc.

You may find APBTs listed for sale in the local paper from time to time. This can be something worth investigating. Many times breeders producing a few litters a year will advertise in a paper. Hold them to the same standards as you would any other breeder, even if they only have a couple of dogs. It is very important to see both parents if you are looking at a puppy. Sometimes, though, you will find that they only have the mother (dam) of the litter there at the house. Ask about going to see the father (sire) as well. The mother is only contributing half of the genetics, so seeing the sire is just as important as seeing the dam. Avoid any advertisement that looks like trouble right from the start, such as ads where the emphasis is on huge size, heavy bone, good guard dog prospects, etc. These people really don't know much about the breed at all.

One way to find someone selling APBTs is to talk to veterinarians. They may know of responsible hobby breeders or even a rescue group in your area. Rescue groups often have older puppies and adults that need homes. Many shelters will euthanize anything that even *resembles* an APBT rather than adopt the dog out. An APBT that has found its way to a rescue group is running short on options. You may be the last shot the APBT has at a home. There is a good chance you will not be given much, if any, background information on a rescue APBT. Many will not have registration papers or a pedigree. The rescue dogs are often spayed or neutered before you get them, so that is potentially one less expense you will have to worry about.

The registration papers on the dog simply show that it is registered with one of the registries. You will need the registration to register a litter of puppies and to show the dog at sanctioned conformation dog shows. There are often "fun shows" where the dogs do not need to be registered to enter. The pedigree is simply a family tree on the dog. You can buy

This striking group of APBTs shows off the many variations of coat color and markings found in the breed. Which one do you like the best?

pedigree forms from many pet stores or mail-order them from pet supply catalogs. If your APBT is registered, the registry can provide a pedigree for a fee. The information on how to get the pedigree should be on the back of the registration papers. Simply having a pedigree does not mean the dog is registered.

A good stainless steel water bowl is a necessity for your APBT. Besides using it to drink from, the water bowl often becomes an APBT's favorite toy!

PREPARING FOR YOUR NEW PUPPY

Before bringing your new APBT home there are some things you will need to have. You will need a heavy collar and leash. APBTs are incredibly strong for their size, especially adults, so it is a good idea to get a heavy-duty leash and collar. There are some places that make collars and leads especially

Wide, heavy collars, like this one, are made especially for strong dogs like the APBT.

*Long-lasting Nylabone®
products are good for
strong chewers like the
APBT. You might want
to start your puppy
with Gumabones®,
which are softer and
easier on puppy teeth.*
for the APBT. You can find people
advertising these in most APBT
magazines. Also, heavy horse leads
make for good leashes for your
APBT. They have heavy snaps and
are made of solid rope.

You will also need both food and
water bowls. If the APBT is going to
be kept outside a lot, then it is a
good idea to get the heavy stainless steel bowls. Many bored
APBTs have chewed up their bowls like chew toys. Not only is
it expensive to constantly replace the bowls, but if large pieces
of the bowl are swallowed it could actually kill your dog. Some
American Pit Bull Terriers will try to chew the stainless steel
bowls as well, so watch for that. They can damage their teeth
this way, and cut their mouths if they puncture the bowls.

Speaking of chew toys, you will want to get some for your
new APBT. There are several on the market that will work for
most dogs, but keep in mind that an APBT has very strong
jaws. Nylabone® produces the toughest and best dog bones for

the APBT. Always buy the largest size possible. For the stronger APBT look for the Hercules™ and Galileo™ bones—guaranteed to last longer than any other dog bone. APBTs can destroy most of the standard chew toys in very little time. There is danger of the APBT swallowing large pieces of a toy and either choking or getting an intestinal blockage. Never give your APBT an old sock or shoe to use as a toy. Some people have been known to do this, but it is just asking for trouble. The new dog will have a hard time figuring out which socks and shoes he can chew on and which ones he can't.

Quality, nutritionally balanced food is important for dogs of all ages. These hungry APBT pups seem to be sharing well at the food bowl!

Find out what kind of food your new APBT has been eating and have it on hand before the dog gets to his new home. The new APBT will be under a bit of stress as he is in a new home, and new food on top of that could really upset the dog's stomach. The different water at the new house could cause the dog a bit of diarrhea, so be patient

with the housebreaking at first. Ask what kinds of treats the dog has been used to and have them on hand as well.

It is also a good idea to have a sturdy dog crate. It should give the dog plenty of room to stand and turn around. The crate is a fantastic tool for housebreaking but is also good to have when you want to travel with your APBT. Plus, you may find there are times you will want to confine your APBT. You may have company who do not like APBTs, or the service man may want you to restrain your dog when you need your meter read. It may make them feel more at ease to see the dog crated rather than to see you just holding him or putting him in another room.

One of the first places you will want to take your new APBT is to the veterinarian's office. Bring with you all the shot and worming records you have. If you stop by the veterinarian's office ahead of time, you can pick up something to collect a stool sample in. You will need a stool sample to check for worms. It is good to take your new APBT to the veterinarian *before* he needs a shot or is sick. If your pet sees a veterinarian only at these times, he may well develop a fear of going. Trust me, a nervous APBT in the waiting room tends to make the others waiting nervous as well!

The most important part of selecting your APBT is remembering that you are choosing a companion and playmate who will bring you happiness for many years!

As an APBT puppy grows, he will change in physical appearance in some ways. As a young pup he will be fat and squat. His ears are often very long for his head. The puppy will be growing very quickly and as he does, he will become very lanky. His legs will seem very long and his head will look a bit more narrow. You can expect your APBT to be a bit lanky from eight months to one year of age. After that, the APBT will start to develop heavy muscles. His head will fill out as well as his back legs. His jaw muscles will really fill in. Even APBTs that are exercised very little will still develop surprising muscularity.

As the APBT matures, you may notice signs of dog aggression. You will need to correct this early if you want to have it under control. Socialize your APBT whenever and wherever possible. Take your APBT to the park, out on walks with you, on picnics, or even on a day of fishing. Not only is it good for your dog, but having a well-mannered APBT in the public eye is good for the image of the breed. Socializing will not keep every APBT from showing some dog aggression at times, but not socializing the dog is guaranteed to cause problems.

This APBT pup will go through many physical changes as he loses his "baby fat" and grows into a lean, muscular adult.

CARING for an APBT

L et's talk about feeding your APBT. Water should be handy for your dog at all times. It is a good idea to limit how much it can drink at one time though, especially for a puppy. A puppy may drink excessively and bloat up. Water can be given to puppies at feeding time only. That is a good idea when you are in the process of housebreaking your new puppy.

There are several good commercial puppy foods out there. Check with both your breeder and veterinarian to see what they recommend. If they like something that may be out of your price range, let them know. You may be surprised at how much some of the specialty dog foods cost! Also check with the veterinarian about any vitamin supplements he would

A balanced diet will help keep your APBT healthy, full of energy, and at a proper weight.

recommend. Let the veterinarian know what you plan to feed the puppy and he may have some ideas for supplements. One warning: you should never feed your puppy from anything but his bowl unless you want your puppy to learn to beg for food later. This will help keep your pup from eating strange things he finds outside. He will only associate eating with his bowl. Little treats and rewards as a training aid are the exception.

I have actually had a dog that ate dog food only from his bowl all his life. Once, I left a sandwich on the coffee table as I answered the phone. The dog looked at the sandwich, sniffed it, and walked away. True story! However, once my father-in-law gave him some table scraps, that ended. He would then take advantage of any chance to get "people food," including once opening the refrigerator! He cleaned out all the lunch meat, cheese, and tortillas.

Your breeder or veterinarian can give you suggestions about what to feed your dog.

If you have a young puppy under four months of age, feed him small meals several times a day. I know that many people like to "free feed" puppies, which is to leave a lot of food down for them to eat as they want it. This makes it a little easier to care for the puppy, but it may not be in the puppy's best interest.

There are two reasons I am against free feeding. First of all, you never know just how much your puppy is eating and when. For instance, if your puppy should catch parvo, you will need to get him to the veterinarian's office as soon as possible. Parvo and coronavirus can kill a puppy in as little as 48 hours. The puppy will need to get to the veterinarian's office right away if there is going to be much hope of saving his life. The first sign of this disease is a loss of appetite. If you are not checking the food regularly, you may not see how much has been eaten. If you only feed your young puppy small meals when you are there, you will know just when any loss of appetite occurs. If there is a loss of appetite, get the pup to the veterinarian's office as soon as you can. If you take your puppy out to public places where there is a lot of "dog traffic," your risk of picking up such a virus is greatly increased.

Secondly, feeding the young puppy several small meals a day keeps him from gorging himself. A young pup may try to eat all the food that you put down no matter how much is there. That will bloat the puppy up and possibly make him vomit or have diarrhea, which is not something you want when you are trying to housebreak a puppy! A good indication that the puppy has had enough to eat is to wait until the puppy has moved away from the food and then to pick up the rest of the food. If you leave the food down, he will come back and eat more. He will learn that you are going to take the food away, so he will eat his fill before moving. If you leave the food down, he will come back and eat to excess.

When the puppy is between four and six months old, switch to feeding three times a day. Stick with a puppy food as you have before. At this age, the puppy is growing very quickly and is very active. Feeding the puppy less than three times a day will leave the puppy very hungry before his next meal. Also, the puppy will have a tendency to overeat at this stage. Once again, leave the food down for him until he moves away from it, then pick it up and give it to him in the next feeding.

From six months of age to maturity, feed the puppy twice a day. At this point, you really shouldn't worry too much about puppy viruses attacking your pup as long as you have kept up on the shots. The young dog is still growing quickly and will be much better off with two separate feedings. Stick with the same foods you have been feeding your puppy. Check with your veterinarian and breeder about any supplements they feel your puppy could use at this phase of life.

After the puppy reaches one year of age you can reduce the feedings down to once a day if you like. At this point free

feeding is an option. If your APBT is very active he will need more food than a "couch potato" would. In the winter it is a good idea to keep your APBT a little on

A little extra weight will help keep your APBT warm if he spends a lot of time outside during the cold winter months.

In warm weather, a lean dog can regulate his body temperature better than an overweight one. Bo is a good example of a fit and trim APBT.

the heavier side, especially if he is going to spend a lot of time outside. This will keep the dog warmer than if he was thin. APBTs kept outside in the cold should have some fat to supplement their diet. In the summer, it is a good idea to keep the APBT a little more on the lean side as this will help him to dissipate heat better. Normally, a healthy APBT will show a lot of definition in his muscles and the outline of the back ribs. You may hear some APBT fanciers say that a heavy dog is "slick." This means that the dog shows very little definition and the coat appears smooth, like the coat of a seal.

When traveling with your American Pit Bull Terrier, it is a good idea to bring along his water and food bowls from home. If you have fed him only from his bowl, he may be hesitant to eat from anything else. His own bowl will be something familiar in a strange place. Also, it is a good idea to bring water from home if you are only going to be gone a day or so. Sometimes the water in a different area will upset the dog's stomach. There is nothing worse on a long trip than a sick dog. If you are going on a long trip with your APBT, take enough water for at least the trip there. This way, if the water does upset his stomach for a bit, you will at least be out of the car. The dog will get used to the water change in time. On the way home it is a good idea to bring some water from where you were (if he has gotten used to it) for the ride home.

GROOMING

The grooming needs of the APBT are minimal. All in all, this is a fairly low-maintenance dog. The nails will need to be clipped when they get too long. If you don't do this, they can break off or split down the middle, which is very

Some dogs take a while to become accustomed to car travel. However, this APBT looks like he's ready to go (but he should probably let his owner do the driving)!

painful for your dog. Even American Pit Bull Terriers, with their high pain tolerance, will be left limping around until the broken nail dies and falls off. Long nails can also cause spreading of the paw if left that way too long. Nail clipping can be done at the veterinarian's office or you can do it at home. Most pet stores carry nail clippers that will do the job. There should be a diagram on the package to show where to clip the nail. Be sure to clip the nails on the dewclaws as well. Be careful when you cut the nails though, because if you cut the nails too short, you will cut into the quick and cause the dog pain and bleeding. This may cause your APBT to try to avoid getting his nails clipped in the future. He may struggle to get away, greatly

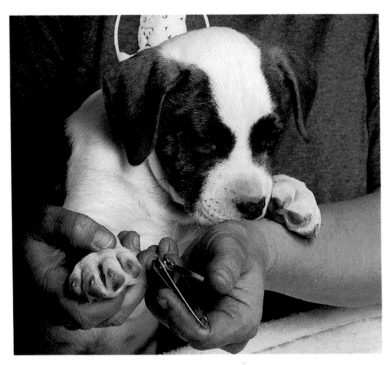

The earlier you start a nail clipping routine with your APBT, the sooner he will be comfortable with the procedure.

improving his chances to get his nails clipped too short once again.

Check the APBT's ears often for dirt and ticks. If you have your dog's ears cropped, there is a greater chance of dirt getting into the ear canal. Clean the ears with cotton swabs and peroxide or alcohol. Be careful not to rub the dog's ears too hard. They may be sensitive, and causing the dog pain will make future cleanings all the more difficult. If you find any black build-up in the dog's ear canal, you will need to treat for ear mites. You can get ear mite medicine from your veterinarian or from most pet stores.

If your APBT stays in the house, bathing him every two weeks will keep him clean. Try to avoid bathing a puppy before the age of three months. If you must bathe such a young puppy, make sure you keep him out of drafts until he is dry. Use mild shampoos or specialty dog shampoos only. Harsh soaps may dry the dog's skin. If you are using a mild soap and your APBT still has a problem with dry skin, you either need to increase the fat in the dog's diet or check the dog for worms. The presence of worms is known to dry out a dog's coat.

An outdoor dog will not need to be bathed as frequently, especially in the winter. An outdoor dog in the winter can go the whole season without being bathed. If you do need to bathe an outdoor dog in the winter, keep him inside until he is dry. This may take a few hours. Some dogs will try to drink some of the water or lick at the soap, but you will want to keep your dog from doing this if he can't be outside for a while. Not only will the dog need to go to the bathroom from drinking water, but the soap may upset the dog's stomach and cause diarrhea—not a good thing for a dog that is going to be in the house for a while!

When bathing your APBT you will want to use lukewarm water. Cold water will chill the dog. Hot water at the same temperature you would bathe in may be uncomfortable for your dog not only during the bath, but also after the bath as the dog will be chilled. You want to make the bathing experience as pleasant as possible for your APBT so he will not come to fear getting a bath.

Always use a mild soap or shampoo to bathe your dog. Remember, harsh soaps will dry out the skin of the dog, especially if you bathe him often. There are many good commercial dog shampoos you can get in most pet stores. Make sure it is a mild shampoo that will not irritate the dog's eyes. Speaking of eyes, you will want to put some petroleum jelly or mineral oil over the dog's eyes to help keep the soap from getting into them. It is a good idea to wash the dog's head with a wash cloth to have better control of where the soap goes, allowing you to better keep it out of the dog's eyes.

EXERCISE

The American Pit Bull Terrier loves physical activity. You will therefore want to exercise your APBT whenever you get the chance. If you don't think you will have the time to exercise your APBT, then you might want to consider another breed. APBTs have been kept as "couch potatoes" but the happiest APBT is the active APBT. This exercise can be fetching sticks in the yard, jogging, hiking, or something more competitive, like weight pulling. A lot of people like taking their APBTs out and letting the dogs pull them around while they rollerblade. Make sure you have a harness for your dog if you are going to do that. You do not want your APBT to have to pull you with a collar.

Biking is something I really don't recommend you do with your APBT. If you have the leash connected to the bike, the dog could very easily pull you over. Remember, the APBT is not the kind of dog that will normally ignore the challenge of another dog. Should a loose dog try to start something, you will have to stop, get off the bike, THEN grab your dog. By that time it may be too late to avoid a scrap. Remember that these dogs have been known to move small cars and mini-vans, so don't think that you will be able to stop a determined APBT while balanced on two wheels!

Is this a water bowl or a wading pool? Piggy knows how to cool down after a vigorous day of play!

Many times APBTs kept outside will actually find ways to exercise themselves. Tossing around the water bowl is very popular! If the dog is kept out near

another dog on a chain or in a kennel, the dogs will often run alongside each other, back and forth to exhaustion. One of the more creative ways, though, is to hang from branches. Many times people will put the APBT out on a chain near a tree so the dog will have shade outside of the doghouse. If there is a branch low enough, the dog may be found swinging from it. There are some APBT shows where "hang time" contests are held. The dog hangs on a piece of rope while the rope is lifted in the air a few feet. "Hang times" between 45 and 60 minutes are fairly common. That sure makes for a long event if you have a lot of dogs entered!

EQUIPMENT

Keeping an APBT as a house dog is easy enough. You will want food and water bowls, leashes, and collars, for starters. You will want a good solid "tie out collar" (wide, buckle type) and also a training collar if you are going to be doing further training with your APBT. The common training collar, often called a "choke chain" or "choke collar" is not really the most effective. You have to remember that the APBT has a very high pain tolerance and may need more force used with this type of collar. You then run the risk of damaging the dog's throat in time. The best results come from the pinch-type collars. I know, they look like some crude, medieval torture device, but

they really are very humane. Instead of a thin chain tightening on the dog's neck, the pinch collar simply pinches the skin of the dog's neck in several places at once. When you pull back on this collar the prongs are pulled together all at once to pinch the skin. Now you would think that "choking" a dog would be more painful, but the APBT seems to respect the pinch a whole lot more! Also with the standard training collar,

APBTs love to hang from branches and ropes—"hang time" contests are common at APBT shows.

which slips over the dog's head, there is the risk of the dog pulling his head out if you don't hold the leash in a way that takes up the slack on the collar. That is something you can avoid easily enough with the pinch-type collar. The pinch collar has links that can be taken out to adjust the collar to just the right size for your dog. Unlike the "choke" style training collar, you can fasten the pinch collar around the dog's neck for a tight fit, making it nearly impossible for your APBT to slip his head out. The pinch

A solid, wide collar and a stainless steel water bowl are two important accessories you will need for your APBT.

A thin collar like this one is often used in the show ring, but should not be used to take your APBT for walks.

collars do cost a bit more, but you have to consider that they can be adjusted to fit several different dogs of different sizes. The "choke" collar will fit different sized dogs as well, as long as you make sure you have it on properly, making sure the slack is always taken up by the weight of the lead.

It is a good idea to also have a crate for your APBT. You will from time to time have guests over that may not like APBTs. As tempting as it may be, we can't always kick out everyone who feels this way! A crate is great for traveling with your APBT. If you are staying in a hotel or with friends, your APBT will appreciate a familiar place to sleep in.

The crate is also one of the best devices for housebreaking your dog. If you make using the crate a positive experience and not a punishment, you may find your APBT will come to think of it as his own private space. Something that works quite well is to give your APBT a little treat every time he has to be crated. Either toss the treat into the crate or give it to him after he gets in. If you do this right from the start, you will find that your dog will race to the crate when you open the door! You will also need a crate if you plan to take your APBT to a dog show. Many shows require that you crate your dog when not in the show ring or participating in a weight pull contest.

A crate will give your APBT his own private space—and will keep him off your furniture!

Fences and kennel runs provide your dog with ample space to exercise and play while making sure he stays in a specified area.

If you have a yard where you plan to let your APBT run, you will need to have a good solid fence—not only to keep your APBT in but also to keep other dogs out. It is a good idea to supervise your APBT when he is loose in the yard. You may be surprised at just how creative your APBT can be when he is looking for a way out. It is not a good idea to use one of those electronic fences. They work with a shock collar that will first sound a warning, then send a little jolt to the dog to keep him inside the "fence." The APBT is known for its incredibly high pain tolerance, making this type of restraint less effective for this breed.

If you plan to have your APBT outside unsupervised, then you will want to look into getting a kennel run for the dog or a good tie-out setup. If you are looking into a kennel run, then you will want to look for one that you can put a top on. APBTs have been known to actually walk right up chain-link fences. I have seen five-week-old APBT pups climb out of a 6-foot-high kennel run! You will want to put either a doghouse in the

kennel or a solid cover over the kennel so the dog can get out of direct sunlight. You will also need some way of locking the gate closed. This will not only keep your APBT from getting out if he figures out the latch, but it will also keep thieves out. There have been enough cases of APBTs being stolen that at least one shelter in Philadelphia refuses to adopt out anything that looks like an APBT. That shelter said the reason was that there had been other "pit bulls" stolen in the past and they were afraid they would be used for fighting.

A car axle makes a good "stake" to anchor the chain in a tie-out setup.

If you are in an area where you feel theft would not be a problem, then you may want to consider a tie-out setup. This most commonly consists of a very heavy snap that is connected to a strong piece of chain, which is in turn connected to an "O" ring (harness ring) which has a "stake" driven through it. One very popular "stake" is a car axle driven into the ground. If the snap has no swivel on it, then you will want to get a very heavy duty swivel to place between the chain and the snap. Each of these components is connected with a "repair link" made for this purpose. Just make sure you get the "O" rings on the axle before you pound it into the ground! This is what you will connect the chain to. Some people bypass the "O" rings altogether and loop the chain tight around the axle, connecting it back to the chain with a repair link. Another variation is to put one or two "O" rings at the end of the chain instead of the snap. Then you can buckle the dog's collar right through the "O" rings. You should be able to pick up everything but the axle at the local hardware store. Getting an axle should be no problem at any area salvage yard.

A good kennel setup has a cover to prevent the dog from climbing out and to provide shade, a locking gate, and a doghouse or other area out of direct sunlight.

You will need to provide your APBT with a good sturdy doghouse if he is to spend much time outside. Even in the warmest areas, the house will need to at least provide shade and a dry place in the rain. There are pre-made doghouses that you can buy in pet stores as well as many hardware stores. If you are handy with simple carpentry tools, then you will be better off making one for yourself. The house should be large enough to allow the dog to stand up and turn around in it with no trouble. A house much larger than this will be too big for your dog's body heat to warm it up. You don't want the opening to come all the way down to the floor of the doghouse. This way, you can better keep bedding material in the doghouse. Straw, old blankets, and cedar shavings make good bedding material. In fact, cedar has been known to help keep the dog free of fleas. It is good to have a roof on the doghouse that is on a hinge so you can open the top for cleaning.

You may never need it, but every APBT owner should have and be able to use a breaking stick.

Every APBT owner should own and know how to use a "breaking stick" (also known as a parting stick). This is the fastest, most humane way of getting an APBT to let go of something, like another APBT! There is a good chance you will never have to use one, but if the need should arise it is best to be prepared.

A breaking stick can be made of any material strong enough to open the dog's jaws, yet still not so hard as to damage the dog's teeth. Plastics and wood are the most common things to make a breaking stick from. A breaking stick usually comes in either the shape of a metal chisel or in the shape of a knife blade. Either style gets the job done.

When you use a breaking stick to get your APBT off something you will first want to straddle your dog. Place your legs tight up against your dog's sides to keep him from moving, then grab a handful of the scruff of the dog's neck with your free hand. Pull the dog's head to the side to expose the side of the dog's mouth. Now work the tip of the breaking stick in between the dog's jaws anywhere behind the dog's incisors (fangs). You should find there is a gap there between the area of the incisors and the molars. You will want to get the tip in about an inch, give or take a little, then twist the breaking stick like you would turn a screwdriver. This will open the dog's mouth, allowing you to back your dog off whatever it has a hold of. Remember to keep the breaking stick in the dog's mouth while you back the dog off, or he may try to grab another hold.

TRAINING Your APBT

American Pit Bull Terriers are highly intelligent. With patience and persistence, you can train the APBT to do most anything. This breed may not be as responsive to verbal commands as are some other breeds, though. Keep in mind that the original purpose of the APBT was to be a fighting dog. There were no verbal commands that the dog had to learn. The APBT was bred to be the top pound-for-pound fighting dog by instinct alone. Contrary to popular myths about dog fighting, there is absolutely *no* training that goes into making a fighting dog, only conditioning to put the dog in top physical shape.

Still, the APBT is a very submissive dog and can be very sensitive. Because of this, harsh training methods are rarely needed. Some examples of the breed may be a bit headstrong and may need more physical correction. If you have a good bond with your APBT, though, this will be the exception. A simple scolding should be enough for basic obedience training.

HOUSEBREAKING

Housebreaking is quite an easy task with a dog crate. The idea behind this method of housebreaking is that a dog will not want to soil his space. If the puppy knows he will be spending a lot of time confined in the crate, he will do his best to avoid any accidents in it. After the first time he goes in the crate and has to be confined with his mess, he will get the idea.

Most any type of crate will work for this. The plastic airline kennels are less expensive, easier to clean, and offer the dog a bit more privacy than the wire mesh

Harsh training methods are usually unnecessary with the intelligent APBT. If your APBT seems a little stubborn, just keep at it!

Crate training is an effective way to housebreak your dog. The fiberglass crates are the safest but the metal crates allow more air.

type. However, the wire mesh type can't be chewed. American Pit Bull Terriers have been known to chew apart the plastic kennels. Not only does this leave you with the loss of the crate but, if the dog swallows pieces of the crate, he could develop an intestinal blockage that could kill him. With either type, it is a good idea to get the optional floor grate. If the puppy has an accident in the kennel, the grate will keep it from getting all over the puppy. Plus, I have found that a layer of cedar under the grate will not only absorb urine and kill some of that urine smell, but will also keep the dog smelling nice. Cedar has been known to help prevent fleas as well.

When getting a crate, make sure that you get one that fits the puppy. It will have to be large enough to allow the puppy to stand and turn around comfortably. Also, the crate should not be so big that the puppy can make a mess at one end, then sleep at the other! This can be a problem when you get a larger crate than is needed, thinking that the dog will be growing and will be outgrowing the crate soon. Some people get larger crates than they need, then use a divider to shorten the length of the crate. This way the same crate can be used later when the puppy is fully grown.

At the start of each morning, take the puppy out right away. If you wait until you have gotten up, made the coffee, and grabbed a snack, the puppy will have already "gone to the bathroom" without you. You will need to get the puppy outside as soon as possible. Praise the puppy for going outside; really lay on the praise as if he is a hero. By giving the puppy so much praise, he will quickly associate going outside with making you happy. Also, the puppy will want to go faster so he can get that praise again. You will come to really appreciate this on cold nights or times when you are running late to get somewhere!

Try to keep a regular schedule of when you take the puppy outside to relieve himself. The puppy will learn that he is going to be taken out at these times and will be more likely to try to control himself than if he never knows when he is going out. Remember to keep with this schedule! If you find an accident in the house after forgetting to take the puppy outside, only blame yourself!

It also is a good idea to take the puppy out to the same place each time. The puppy will be able to smell where he has gone before and will associate this with going there again. That is why it is so very important to clean up any accidents in the house with something that will kill the odor. If the puppy smells his urine on the carpet where he has had an accident in the past, he will most likely go there again. Club soda or pine-scented disinfectants work great for urine spots.

The puppy will also need to be taken out after every meal and after any playtime. If you play with your puppy inside and forget to take him out right away, you have no one to blame for any accidents but yourself. Keep in mind that a puppy between 8 and 12 weeks of age will need to be let out as often as every two hours. As the puppy matures, he will gain better control of his bladder and bowels.

If you are crate training, then you will want to keep the puppy in the crate any time you can't be there to supervise. It helps to give the puppy a little treat and to praise him for going into the crate. This will help the puppy to think of the crate as something positive and you will find the puppy racing to the crate when he sees you open the door! Puppies sleep a lot, and in a home with small children this will give the puppy some quiet time away from the kids to catch up on his rest. When you see the puppy has awakened from a long nap, you will want to get him outside right away. The puppy may start whining at this point to let you know that he is in danger of messing up his bed.

For people who live in apartments where it is not all that easy to get the puppy outside, paper training is an option. This is where the puppy is placed on newspapers instead of taken outside when nature calls. Soon the puppy will associate the papers with "going to the bathroom." It is best to keep the papers on a tile or linoleum surface. This makes cleanup a whole lot easier. Also, keeping the papers close to the door helps the puppy to associate going to the door with going to the bathroom. When you clean up the papers, it is a good idea to keep one of the soiled papers to use with the fresh paper. This will let the puppy smell where he has been before and therefore

Paper training is another commonly used method of housebreaking. Here is Bonehead and a littermate at around five weeks of age.

associate the papers with eliminating. It is also helpful when taking a paper-trained puppy outside to take a soiled paper with you. Place the soiled paper on the ground where you want the puppy to go. Again, the smell will help the puppy to figure out what you want him to do.

Every puppy is going to have some accidents in the house. More times than not, this is the fault of the owner. Either the owner hasn't conveyed to the puppy just what is expected or the owner hasn't had the puppy out often enough. If you catch the puppy in the act, then correct him with a harsh "no!" and take him outside immediately. If you find a mess and don't know when it was made, just clean it up. The memory of a young puppy is only around 30 seconds long. If the accident happened longer ago than that, the puppy will have no idea why he is being corrected. Again, when you clean the mess up, make sure to do it thoroughly enough that there will be no scent left for the puppy to return to.

In time, you will learn the signs your puppy makes when he needs to go outside. The puppy may start to anxiously sniff around more than usual. He may run back and forth to the door as if he is looking for something. When you see the signs, drop whatever you are doing and get the puppy outside or on the papers as quickly as possible. Each time the puppy is forced to relieve himself in the house, it takes that much longer to housebreak him.

TRAINING TIPS

Before talking about other types of training for your APBT, there are some simple guidelines to follow that will help make the training not only more enjoyable for your dog, but more effective. First and foremost, *never* train your APBT when you are in a bad mood. You are far more likely to lose your patience and be too hard on your dog. If you lose control of your emotions and become abusive, your APBT will become frightened and lose confidence in you. Don't let the training last so long that the dog becomes bored. You don't accomplish anything when your dog is no longer paying attention to you, and you will just be frustrating yourself. Keep the sessions short and fun so your APBT looks forward to this time together. The best time to train is after your APBT has had some rest. Some will crate the dog for a time before training so that the APBT is more alert and looking forward to being out and about. Also, it is a good idea to hold training sessions before feeding the dog. This way, your APBT will be working harder to get a treat. The dog may become a bit lethargic after a big meal and not take much interest in training.

You can start training your APBT puppy in simple obedience as early as three months. Before that it is best to just let the little one enjoy being a puppy. More complicated training should wait until the puppy is at least six months of age. Again, let the puppy be a puppy! Simple obedience should include such things as sit, down, stay, and come. You should have no problem teaching these commands to a young dog. Always use the same commands. If you change the name of the command, you will only confuse your dog. You should start with short 5- to 10-minute training sessions with the young dog, while sessions up to 20 minutes are fine for the adult APBT.

Keep training sessions with your APBT short and fun so that you hold your dog's attention.

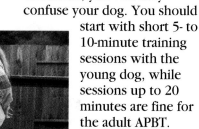

TRAINING FOR WEIGHT PULLING

Weight pulling is something else you may want to consider training your APBT to do. It is a great physical activity that will really build up the strength of your APBT. Plus, your dog can compete in weight pull events and at shows. If you want to start with a younger pup, keep the weight light. Wait until the APBT has fully developed before having him pull any serious weight. No APBTs under the age of nine months are allowed to enter an ADBA weight pull event.

First, you will need to get a good weight pull harness. Most of the APBT specialty magazines as well as some of the general dog magazines will have advertisers that sell these. Many APBT shows will have vendors present that offer weight pull harnesses. If ordering one through the mail, you will need to provide information on the size of your dog. Usually they determine the size of the harness by the weight of the dog, while some will want actual measurements for a custom fit.

Once you have the harness, let the dog check it out. You want your APBT to be comfortable with having this new contraption placed on him! Take the dog for walks with the harness on and let him get used to how it feels. After your dog is comfortable with the harness, start adding some weight. You will need to get a piece of chain and attach a heavy snap to each end. This is how you will attach the weight. Window weights work well because you can add weight in small increments. Simply attach a snap to the end of the window weight and connect it to the chain.

Start taking the dog for walks with light weight at first. Always remember to walk the dog in the grass! You don't want the dog trying to pull weight on asphalt or concrete.

Once your APBT is used to pulling weight with the harness, you can start

Your APBT should be comfortable with his harness before any weight is added. Here, Diamond C's Mako models his weight-pull harness.

Just a few more feet...This APBT is determined to finish his pull. with short pulls with heavier weight. The ADBA weight pull events have a pulling distance of 15 feet, so distances of at least 15 feet are good for your training pulls if you wish to compete in these events. You may want to use a training distance of 16 feet so your APBT gets used to pulling the weight over the 15-foot mark. Attach the weight to the harness, then have the dog "stay." Walk in front of the dog and give him the command to pull. The commands "pull" and "work" are the most popular. You can attach a lead to the dog to get him started. Remember that in actual events you will not be allowed to touch the dog so you will want him to get used to doing it on his own. After your APBT has pulled the distance, praise him and let him have a rest. In a weight pull event, there will be at least a five-minute rest period before your dog is allowed to pull again.

When doing the short pulls with heavy weights, once again, stay on a soft surface. You can do this in the grass or use a piece of old carpet. Most of the sanctioned weight pull tracks will be carpeted so you may want to get the dog used to this.

You can use just about anything for the weight that will not snag on the ground. Some have had good luck with big plastic jugs filled with water, actual weightlifting weight plates, and even old tires. If you plan to be a serious competitor you may want to devise a cart like the kind that is actually used in the events.

TRAINING FOR GUARD WORK

American Pit Bull Terriers can also be trained to be protection and guard dogs. APBTs are known to be protective of their families when they have to be *without* any training. If you want to train your APBT in guard work, be prepared

Loyal APBTs are naturally protective of their human families without additional training in guard work.

to spend a good amount of money and time with a professional trainer. To bite a person goes against what the APBT has been bred countless generations for. When you look at all of the time and money it will take to properly make a guard dog out of your APBT, you may find it better to just buy a dog of a breed that excels at this work naturally.

Beware of "trainers" who take shortcuts in training an APBT in bitework. These people will abuse your dog to the point where he is simply defending himself. In this way, the APBT will be taught that all strangers are potential attackers. At this point, your APBT should not be trusted out in public because the poor animal is simply trying to defend himself against everybody. A dog like this is just as likely to attack a friend as he is to attack an intruder. He will have to remain restrained most of the time, which means he cannot be there to defend you or your property. It is because of dogs like this that APBTs have gotten such a bad reputation.

Weight pulling is a strenuous activity—this young APBT is exhausted just from watching.

SPORT of Purebred Dogs

Welcome to the exciting and sometimes frustrating sport of dogs. No doubt you are trying to learn more about dogs or you wouldn't be deep into this book. This section covers the basics that may entice you, further your knowledge and help you to understand the dog world. If you decide to give showing, obedience or any other dog activities a try, then I suggest you seek further help from the appropriate source.

Dog showing has been a very popular sport for a long time and has been taken quite seriously by some. Others only enjoy it as a hobby.

These APBT pups may look cute and innocent, but they still need some basic obedience training to help keep them out of trouble!

Today there are numerous activities that are enjoyable for both the dog and the handler. Some of the activities include conformation showing, obedience competition, tracking, agility, the Canine Good Citizen Certificate, and a wide range of instinct tests that vary from breed to breed. Where you start depends upon your goals which early on may not be readily apparent.

PUPPY KINDERGARTEN

Every puppy will benefit from this class. PKT is the foundation for all future dog activities from conformation to "couch potatoes." Pet owners should make an effort to attend even if they never expect to show their dog. The class is designed for puppies about three months of age with

In puppy kindergarten classes, the owner learns how to teach his dog certain commands. Here, the trainer guides the dog into the "down" position.

graduation at approximately five months of age. All the puppies will be in the same age group and, even though some may be a little unruly, there should not be any real problem. This class will teach the puppy some beginning obedience. As in all obedience classes the owner learns how to train his own dog. The PKT class gives the puppy the opportunity to interact with other puppies in the same age group and exposes him to strangers, which is very important. Some dogs grow up with behavior problems, one of them being fear of strangers. As you can see, there can be much to gain from this class.

There are some basic obedience exercises that every dog should learn. Some of these can be started with puppy kindergarten.

Sit

One way of teaching the sit is to have your dog on your left side with the leash in your right hand, close to the collar. Pull up on the leash and at the same time reach around his hindlegs with your left hand and tuck them in. As you are doing this say, "Beau, sit." Always use the dog's name when you give an active command. Some owners like to use a treat holding it over the dog's head. The dog will need to sit to get the treat. Encourage the dog to hold the sit for a few seconds, which will eventually be the beginning of the Sit/Stay. Depending on how cooperative he is, you can rub him under the chin or stroke his back. It is a good time to establish eye contact.

Down

Sit the dog on your left side and kneel down beside him with the leash in your right hand. Reach over him with your left hand and grasp his left foreleg. With your right hand, take his right foreleg and pull his legs forward while you say, "Beau, down." If he tries to get up, lean on his shoulder to encourage him to stay down. It will relax your dog if you stroke his back while he is down. Try to encourage him to stay down for a few seconds as preparation for the Down/Stay.

Heel

The definition of heeling is the dog walking under control at your left heel. Your puppy will learn controlled walking in the puppy kindergarten class, which will eventually lead to heeling. The command is "Beau, heel," and you start off briskly

The trainer pulls up on the dog's leash while tucking his hind legs under. The result—the perfect sit followed by lots of praise!

with your left foot. Your leash is in your right hand and your left hand is holding it about half way down. Your left hand should be able to control the leash and there should be a little slack in it. You want him to walk with you with your leg somewhere between his nose and his shoulder. You need to encourage him to stay with you, not forging (in front of you) or lagging behind you. It is best to keep him on a fairly short lead. Do not allow the lead to become tight. It is far better to give him a little jerk when necessary and remind him to heel. When you come to a halt, be

Down is another basic obedience command. Here, the trainer starts the dog in the sit position and coaxes him into the down.

It is very important for your dog to learn how to heel so that he will walk at a controlled pace on a leash.

prepared physically to make him sit. It takes practice to become coordinated. There are excellent books on training that you may wish to purchase. Your instructor should be able to recommend one for you.

Recall

This quite possibly is the most important exercise you will ever teach. It should be a pleasant experience. The puppy may learn to do random recalls while being attached to a long line such as a clothes line. Later the exercise will start with the dog sitting and staying until called. The command is "Beau, come." Let your command be happy. You want your dog to come willingly and faithfully. The recall could save his life if he sneaks out the door. In practicing the recall, let him jump on you or touch you before you reach for him. If he is shy, then kneel down to his level. Reaching for the insecure dog could frighten him, and he may not be willing to come again in the future. Lots of praise and a treat would be in order whenever you do a recall. Under no circumstances should you ever correct your dog when he has come to you. Later in formal obedience your dog will be required to sit in front of you after recalling and then go to heel position.

By using a pleasant, friendly tone of voice when practicing the recall, your dog will happily respond to your command.

After a productive training session, always remember to reward your dog with a lot of praise and perhaps a tasty treat!

CONFORMATION

Conformation showing is our oldest dog show sport. This type of showing is based on the dog's appearance—that is his structure, movement and attitude. When considering this type of showing, you need to be aware of your breed's standard and be able to evaluate your dog compared to that standard. The breeder of your puppy or other experienced breeders would be good sources for such an evaluation. Puppies can go through lots of changes over a period of time. I always say most puppies start out as promising hopefuls and then after maturing may be disappointing as show candidates. Even so this should not deter them from being excellent pets.

Usually conformation training classes are offered by the local kennel or obedience clubs. These are excellent places for training puppies. The puppy should be able to walk on a lead before entering such a class. Proper ring procedure and technique for posing (stacking) the dog will be demonstrated as well as gaiting the dog. Usually certain patterns are used in the ring such as the triangle or the "L." Conformation class, like the PKT class, will give your youngster the opportunity to socialize with different breeds of dogs and humans too.

It takes some time to learn the routine of conformation showing. The American Dog Breeders Association (ADBA) and the United Kennel Club (UKC) are two organizations which sponsor conformation shows for the APBT. These shows are organized in a similar fashion to those of the American Kennel Club (AKC), but are usually more relaxed and informal. Both groups offer puppy and adult classes, so you can start familiarizing your APBT with the conformation show ring at an early age.

A few matches can be great training for puppies even though there is no intention to go on showing. Matches enable the puppy to meet new people and be handled by a stranger—the judge. It is also a change of environment, which broadens the horizon for both dog and handler. Matches and other dog activities boost the confidence of the handler and especially the younger handlers.

At an ADBA conformation show, the dogs are divided into classes based on age and sex. Males and females compete separately in the following age categories: 4 to 6 months, 6 to 9 months, 9 to 12 months, 12 to 18 months, 18 to 24 months, 2 to 3 years, 3 to 5 years, and 5 years and older. Puppies must be at least four months old in order to be eligible for competition.

It takes some time for both dog and owner to get used to the routine of conformation showing. Here, the handler presents the dog's mouth for examination.

Earning an ADBA championship is based on a point system. In the puppy classes, first place is awarded five points, second place is awarded three points, and third place is awarded two points. If the puppy wins over at least ten other puppies in the class, the point values increase to eight points for first place, five points for second place, and three points for third place. In the adult classes, first place is awarded ten points, second place is awarded five points, and third place is awarded three points. Again, if the dog wins over at least ten other dogs, the point values increase— 15 points for first place, eight points for second place, and five points for third

In conformation showing, APBTs are evaluated on how closely they resemble the breed standard, or picture of the ideal APBT.

place. A Best of Show win carries 15 points, and the Best of Opposite Sex and the Best Puppy each receive ten points.

A dog must accumulate 100 points in order to earn the Champion title, and there is no time limit for him to do this. Once a dog has become a champion, he is eligible to compete in the Champion of Champions class against other champion-titled dogs. In this class, first place is awarded 15 points, second place is awarded ten points, and third place is awarded five points. The Champion title is the only title available to APBTs in ADBA conformation, however, every additional 100 points that a dog accumulates after becoming a champion raises him to a higher degree of championship status.

The UKC shows are also based on a point system, and the dogs are also divided into classes according to age and sex. Males and females compete separately in each of the following classes: Puppy (must be at least six months old but less than one year old), Junior (must be at least one year old but less than two years old), Senior (must be at least two years old but less than three years old), and Veteran (three years old and older). A win in any of these classes is worth five points. The Best Male and Best Female in Show are chosen from these winners, and they each receive ten points. The Best in Show winner receives 12 points. Dogs who have already earned either the Show Champion (Ch.) or Grand Show Champion

(Gr.Ch.) title can compete in either the Champion of Champions class or the Grand Champions class.

A dog earns the Show Champion title by having a minimum of 100 points earned under at least three different judges, and by having at least one Best Male or Best Female ("major") win. The Grand Show Champion title is earned by having at least three Champion of Champions wins under at least three different judges.

Typically, the handlers are very particular about their appearances. They are careful not to wear something that will detract from their dog but will perhaps enhance it. American ring procedure is quite formal compared to that of other countries. I remember being reprimanded by a judge because I made a suggestion to a friend holding my second dog outside the ring. I certainly could have used more discretion so I would not call attention to myself. There is a certain etiquette expected between the judge and exhibitor and among the other exhibitors. Of course it is not always the case but the judge is supposed to be polite, not engaging in small talk or even acknowledging that he knows the handler. I understand that there is a more informal and relaxed atmosphere at the shows in other countries. For instance, the dress code is more casual. I can see where this might be more fun for the exhibitor and especially for the novice. This country is very handler-oriented in many of the breeds. It is true, in most instances, that the experienced professional handler can present the dog better and will have a feel for what a judge likes.

A dog must become accustomed to standing still while being examined by the conformation judge.

If you are handling your own dog, please give some consideration to your apparel. For sure the dress code at matches is more informal than the point shows. However, you should wear something a little more appropriate than beach attire or ragged jeans and bare feet. If you check out the handlers and see what is presently fashionable, you'll catch on. Men usually dress with a shirt and tie and a nice sports coat. Whether you are male or female, you will want to wear comfortable clothes and shoes. You need to be able to run with your dog and you certainly don't want to take a chance of falling and hurting yourself. Heaven forbid, if nothing else,

you'll upset your dog. Women usually wear a dress or two-piece outfit, preferably with pockets to carry bait, comb, brush, etc. In this case men are the lucky ones with all their pockets. Ladies, think about where your dress will be if you need to kneel on the floor and also think about running. Does it allow freedom to do so?

Years ago, after toting around all the baby paraphernalia, I found toting the dog and necessities a breeze. You need to take along dog; crate; ex pen (if you use one); extra newspaper; water pail and water; all required grooming equipment, including hair dryer and extension cord; table; chair for you; bait for dog and lunch for you and friends; and, last but not least, clean up materials, such as plastic bags, paper towels, and perhaps a bath towel and some shampoo—just in case. Don't forget your entry confirmation and directions to the show.

This APBT puppy needs a rest from all of the excitement at a dog show. Notice the thin collar and lead, which is commonly seen in the show ring.

If you are showing in obedience, then you will want to wear pants. Many of our top obedience handlers wear pants that are color-coordinated with their dogs. The philosophy is that imperfections in the black dog will be less obvious next to your black pants.

Whether you are showing in conformation, or obedience, you need to watch the clock and be sure you are not late. It is customary to pick up your conformation armband a few minutes before the start of the class. They will not wait for you and if you are on the show grounds and not in the ring, you will upset everyone. It's a little more complicated picking up your obedience armband if you show later in the class. If you

Wide leashes and harness are specially made for walking strong dogs like the APBT, but they are usually not worn in the show ring.

have not picked up your armband and they get to your number, you may not be allowed to show. It's best to pick up your armband early, but then you may show earlier than expected if other handlers don't pick up. Customarily all conflicts should be discussed with the judge prior to the start of the class.

Canine Good Citizen

The AKC sponsors a program to encourage dog owners to train their dogs. Local clubs perform the pass/fail tests, and dogs who pass are awarded a Canine Good Citizen Certificate. Proof of vaccination is required at the time of participation. The test includes:
1. Accepting a friendly stranger.
2. Sitting politely for petting.
3. Appearance and grooming.
4. Walking on a loose leash.
5. Walking through a crowd.
6. Sit and down on command/staying in place.
7. Come when called.
8. Reaction to another dog.
9. Reactions to distractions.
10. Supervised separation.

If more effort was made by pet owners to accomplish these exercises, fewer dogs would be cast off to the humane shelter.

Obedience

Obedience is necessary, without a doubt, but it can also become a wonderful hobby or even an obsession. In my opinion, obedience classes and competition can provide wonderful companionship, not only with your dog but with your classmates or fellow competitors. It is always gratifying to discuss your dog's problems with others who have had similar experiences. The AKC acknowledged Obedience around 1936, and it has changed tremendously even though many of the exercises are basically the same. Today, obedience competition is just that—very competitive. Even so, it is possible for every obedience exhibitor to come home a winner (by earning qualifying scores) even though he/she may not earn a placement in the class. Although the APBT is not an AKC-registered breed, it is eligible to compete in and earn titles in AKC-

To become a Canine Good Citizen, a dog must be able to react well to strangers and sit for petting, among other things. This APBT is well on his way to passing the test!

"Can we get up now?" The down-stay is hard enough without the distraction of a nearby gaggle of baby geese, but these well-trained APBTs are doing a fine job.

sanctioned events other than conformation.

Most of the obedience titles are awarded after earning three qualifying scores (legs) in the appropriate class under three different judges. These classes offer a perfect score of 200, which is extremely rare. Each of the class exercises has its own point value. A leg is earned after receiving a score of at least 170 and at least 50 percent of the points available in each exercise. The titles are:

Companion Dog—CD

This is called the Novice Class and the exercises are:

1. Heel on leash and figure 8	40 points
2. Stand for examination	30 points
3. Heel free	40 points
4. Recall	30 points
5. Long sit—one minute	30 points
6. Long down—three minutes	30 points
Maximum total score	200 points

Companion Dog Excellent–CDX
This is the Open Class and the exercises are:

1. Heel off leash and figure 8	40 points
2. Drop on recall	30 points
3. Retrieve on flat	20 points
4. Retrieve over high jump	30 points
5. Broad jump	20 points
6. Long sit–three minutes (out of sight)	30 points
7. Long down–five minutes (out of sight)	30 points
Maximum total score	200 points

Utility Dog–UD
The Utility Class exercises are:

1. Signal Exercise	40 points
2. Scent discrimination-Article 1	30 points
3. Scent discrimination-Article 2	30 points
4. Directed retrieve	30 points
5. Moving stand and examination	30 points
6. Directed jumping	40 points
Maximum total score	200 points

After achieving the UD title, you may feel inclined to go after the UDX and/or OTCh. The UDX (Utility Dog Excellent) title went into effect in January 1994. It is not easily attained. The title requires qualifying simultaneously ten times in Open B and Utility B but not necessarily at consecutive shows.

The OTCh (Obedience Trial Champion) is awarded after the dog has earned his UD and then goes on to earn 100

This APBT practices the broad jump, a required exercise in the obedience Open Class.

88

championship points, a first place in Utility, a first place in Open and another first place in either class. The placements must be won under three different judges at all-breed obedience trials. The points are determined by the number of dogs competing in the Open B and Utility B classes. The OTCh title precedes the dog's name.

Scent discrimination is an obedience Utility Class exercise. The dog must locate out of a group of articles which ones have the handler's scent.

Obedience matches (AKC Sanctioned, Fun, and Show and Go) are usually available. Usually they are sponsored by the local obedience clubs. When preparing an obedience dog for a title, you will find matches very helpful. Fun Matches and Show and Go Matches are more lenient in allowing you to make corrections in the ring. I frequently train (correct) in the ring and inform the judge that I would like to do so and to please mark me "exhibition." This means that I will not be eligible for any prize. This type of training is usually very necessary for the Open and Utility Classes. AKC Sanctioned Obedience Matches do not allow corrections in the ring since they must abide by the AKC Obedience Regulations. If you are interested in showing in obedience, then you should contact the AKC for a copy of the Obedience Regulations.

TRACKING

Tracking is officially classified obedience, but I feel it should have its own category. There are three tracking titles available: Tracking Dog (TD), Tracking Dog Excellent (TDX), Variable Surface Tracking (VST). If all three tracking titles are obtained, then the dog officially becomes a CT (Champion Tracker). The CT will go in front of the dog's name.

A TD may be earned anytime and does not have to follow the other obedience titles. There are many exhibitors that prefer tracking to obedience, and there are others like myself that do both. In my experience with small dogs, I prefer to earn the CD and CDX before attempting tracking. My reasoning is that small dogs are closer to the mat in the obedience rings and therefore it's too easy to put the nose down and sniff. Tracking encourages sniffing. Of course this depends on the dog. I've had some dogs that tracked around the ring and others (TDXs) who wouldn't think of sniffing in the ring.

AGILITY

Agility was first introduced by John Varley in England at the Crufts Dog Show, February 1978, but Peter Meanwell, competitor and judge, actually developed the idea. It was officially recognized in the early '80s. Agility is extremely popular in England and Canada and growing in popularity in the U.S. The AKC acknowledged agility in August 1994. Dogs must be at least 12 months of age to be entered. It is a fascinating sport that the dog, handler and spectators enjoy to the utmost. Agility is a spectator sport! The dog performs off lead. The handler either runs with his dog or positions himself on the course and directs his dog with verbal and hand signals over a timed course over or through a variety of obstacles including a time out or pause. One of the main drawbacks to agility is finding a place to train. The obstacles take up a lot of space and it is very time consuming to put up and take down courses.

The titles earned at AKC agility trials are Novice Agility Dog (NAD), Open Agility Dog (OAD), Agility Dog Excellent (ADX), and Master Agility Excellent (MAX). In order to acquire an agility title, a dog must earn a qualifying score in its respective class on three separate occasions under two different judges. The MAX will be awarded after earning ten qualifying scores in the Agility Excellent Class.

PERFORMANCE TESTS

During the last decade the American Kennel Club has promoted performance tests—those events that test the different breeds' natural abilities. This type of event encourages a handler to devote even more time to his dog and retain the natural instincts of his breed heritage. It is an important part of the wonderful world of dogs. The APBT is considered one of the most versatile and talented of all breeds. Although many of the following events are geared toward specific types of dogs, the APBT, when permitted in these events, has consistently fared well and enjoyed tremendous success.

Lure Coursing

For all sighthounds (Afghans, Basenjis, Borzois, Greyhounds, Ibizans, Irish Wolfhounds, Pharaoh Hounds, Rhodesian Ridgebacks, Salukis, Scottish Deerhounds, and Whippets).

The participant must be at least one year of age, and dogs with limited registration (ILP) are elgible. They chase a lure of three plastic bags and are judged on overall ability, follow, speed, agility and endurance. Like the other AKC performance tests, lure coursing gives dogs the opportunity to prove themselves at what they were originally bred to do.

Junior Courser (JC) A hound running alone shall receive certification from a judge on one date, and a second certification at a later time, stating the hound completed a 600-yard course with a minimum of four turns. The hound must complete the course with enthusiasm and without interruption.

Agility is a fun and popular sport for dogs and spectators alike! Dogs must complete a timed course comprised of obstacles like the A-frame in the background.

Senior Courser (SC) Must be elgible to enter the open stake and the hound must run with at least one other hound. Must receive qualifying scores at four AKC-licensed or member trials under two different judges.

Field Championship (FC) Prefix to the hound's name. Must receive 15 championship points including two first placements with three points or more under two different judges.

Earthdog Events

For small terriers (Australian, Bedlington, Border, Cairn, Dandie Dinmont, Fox (Smooth & Wire), Lakeland, Norfolk, Norwich, Scottish, Sealyham, Skye, Welsh, West Highland White and Dachshunds).

Limited registration (ILP) dogs are eligible and all entrants must be at least six months of age. The primary purpose of the small terriers and Dachshunds is to pursue quarry to ground, hold the game, and alert the hunter where to dig, or to bolt. There are two parts to the test: (1) the approach to the quarry and (2) working the quarry. The dog must pass both parts for a Junior Earthdog (JE). The Senior Earthdog (SE) must do a third part—to leave the den on command. The Master Earthdog (ME) is a bit more complicated.

Hunting Titles
For retrievers, pointing breeds and spaniels. Titles offered are Junior Hunter (JH), Senior Hunter (SH), and Master Hunter (MH).

Flushing Spaniels Their primary purpose is to hunt, find, flush and return birds to hand as quickly as possible in a pleasing and obedient manner. The entrant must be at least six months of age and dogs with limited registration (ILP) are eligible. Game used are pigeons, pheasants, and quail.

Retrievers Limited registration (ILP) retrievers are not eligible to compete in Hunting Tests. The purpose of a Hunting Test for retrievers is to test the merits of and evaluate the abilities of retrievers in the field in order to determine their suitability and ability as hunting companions. They are expected to retrieve any type of game bird, pheasants, ducks, pigeons, guinea hens and quail.

Pointing Breeds Are eligible at six months of age, and dogs with limited registration (ILP) are permitted. They must show a keen desire to hunt; be bold and independent; have a fast, yet attractive, manner of hunting; and demonstrate intelligence not only in seeking objectives but also in the ability to find game. They must establish point, and in the more advanced tests they need to be steady to wing and must remain in position until the bird is shot or they are released.

A Senior Hunter must retrieve. A Master Hunter must honor. The judges and the marshal are permitted to ride horseback during the test, but all handling must be done on foot.

Herding Titles
For all Herding breeds and Rottweilers and Samoyeds. Entrants must be at least nine months of age and dogs with

limited registration (ILP) are eligible. The Herding program is divided into Testing and Trial sections. The goal is to demonstrate proficiency in herding livestock in diverse situations. The titles offered are Herding Started (HS), Herding Intermediate (HI), and Herding Excellent (HX). Upon completion of the HX a Herding Championship may be earned after accumulating 15 championship points.

The above information has been taken from the AKC Guidelines for the appropriate events.

SCHUTZHUND

The German word "Schutzhund" translated to English means "Protection Dog." It is a fast growing competitive sport in the United States and has been popular in England since the early 1900s. Schutzhund was originally a test to determine which German Shepherds were quality dogs for breeding in Germany.

APBTs often fare well in Schutzhund competition, with many of them earning advanced titles. It gives us the ability to test our dogs for correct temperament and working ability. Like every other dog sport, it requires teamwork between the handler and the dog.

Schutzhund training and showing involves three phases: Tracking, Obedience and Protection. There are three SchH levels: SchH

I (novice), SchH II (intermediate), and SchH III (advanced). Each title becomes progressively more difficult. The handler and dog start out in each phase with 100 points. Points are deducted as errors are incurred. A total perfect score is 300, and for a dog and handler to earn a title he must earn at least 70 points in tracking and obedience and at least 80 points in protection. Today many different breeds participate successfully in Schutzhund.

There are so many activities that you and your APBT can participate in together. Consider all of the options—the versatile APBT is suited to them all!

GENERAL INFORMATION

Information about conformation showing for the APBT can be obtained from the ADBA and the UKC. Information about obedience trials and other areas of competition is available through the AKC. Frequently these events are not superintended, but put on by the host club. Therefore you would make the entry with the event's host club. Therefore you would make the entry with the event's secretary. Following are the addresses of the various kennel clubs should you wish to request further information.

The American Kennel Club
51 Madison Avenue
New York, NY 10010

The American Dog Breeders Association
Box 1771
Salt Lake City, UT 84110

The United Kennel Club
100 E. Kilgore Rd.
Kalamazoo, MI 49001

As you have read, there are numerous activities you can share with your dog. Regardless what you do, it does take teamwork. Your dog can only benefit from your attention and training. I hope this chapter has enlightened you and hope, if nothing else, you will attend a show here and there. Perhaps you will start with a puppy kindergarten class, and who knows where it may lead!

HEALTH CARE

eterinary medicine has become far more sophisticated than what was available to our ancestors. This can be attributed to the increase in household pets and consequently the demand for better care for them. Also human medicine has become far more complex. Today diagnostic testing in veterinary medicine parallels human diagnostics. Because of better technology we can expect our pets to live healthier lives thereby increasing their life spans.

This young APBT pup has a lot of potential! Proper health care right from the start ensures that he will be able to lead a full, active life.

THE FIRST CHECK UP

You will want to take your new puppy/dog in for its first check up within 48 to 72 hours after acquiring it. Many breeders strongly recommend this check up and so do the humane shelters. A puppy/dog can appear healthy but it may have a serious problem that is not apparent to the layman. Most pets have some type of a minor flaw that may never cause a real problem.

Unfortunately if he/she should have a serious problem, you will want to consider the consequences of keeping the pet and the attachments that will be formed, which may be broken prematurely. Keep in mind there are many healthy dogs looking for good homes.

This first check up is a good time to establish yourself with the veterinarian and learn the office policy regarding their hours and how they handle emergencies. Usually the breeder or another conscientious pet owner is a good reference for locating a capable veterinarian. You should be aware that not all veterinarians give the same quality of service. Please do not make your selection on the least expensive clinic, as they may be short changing your pet. There is the possibility that eventually it will cost you more due to improper diagnosis, treatment, etc. If you are selecting a new veterinarian, feel free to ask for a tour of the clinic. You should inquire about making

an appointment for a tour since all clinics are working clinics, and therefore may not be available all day for sightseers. You may worry less if you see where your pet will be spending the day if he ever needs to be hospitalized.

THE PHYSICAL EXAM

Your veterinarian will check your pet's overall condition, which includes listening to the heart; checking the respiration; feeling the abdomen, muscles and joints; checking the mouth, which includes the gum color and signs of gum disease along with plaque buildup; checking the ears for signs of an infection or ear mites; examining the eyes; and, last but not least, checking the condition of the skin and coat.

Vaccinations are necessary to protect your dog from potentially life-threatening diseases. Your veterinarian can set up a vaccination schedule for your APBT puppy.

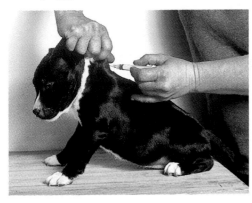

He should ask you questions regarding your pet's eating and elimination habits and invite you to relay your questions. It is a good idea to prepare a list so as not to forget anything. He should discuss the proper diet and the quantity to be fed. If this should differ from your breeder's recommendation, then you should convey to him the breeder's choice and see if he approves. If he recommends changing the diet, then this should be done over a few days so as not to cause a gastrointestinal upset. It is customary to take in a fresh stool sample (just a small amount) for a test for intestinal parasites. It must be fresh, preferably within 12 hours, since the eggs hatch quickly and after hatching will not be observed under the microscope. If your pet isn't obliging then, usually the technician can take one in the clinic.

Puppies receive maternal antibodies that protect them from disease for their first few weeks of life.

IMMUNIZATIONS

It is important that you take your puppy/dog's vaccination record with you on your first visit. In case of a puppy, presumably the breeder has seen to the vaccinations up to the time you acquired custody. Veterinarians differ in their vaccination protocol. It is not unusual for your puppy to have received vaccinations for distemper, hepatitis, leptospirosis, parvovirus and parainfluenza every two to three weeks from the age of five or six weeks. Usually this is a combined injection and is typically called the DHLPP. The DHLPP is given through at least 12 to 14 weeks of age, and it is customary to continue with another parvovirus vaccine at 16 to 18 weeks. You may wonder why so many immunizations are necessary. No one knows for sure when the puppy's maternal antibodies are gone, although it is customarily accepted that distemper antibodies are gone by 12 weeks. Usually parvovirus antibodies are gone by 16 to 18 weeks of age. However, it is possible for the maternal antibodies to be gone at a much earlier age or even a later age. Therefore immunizations are started at an early age. The vaccine will not give immunity as long as there are maternal antibodies.

The rabies vaccination is given at three or six months of age depending on your local laws. A vaccine for bordetella (kennel cough) is advisable and can be given anytime from the age of five weeks. The coronavirus is not commonly given unless there is a problem locally. The Lyme vaccine is necessary in endemic areas. Lyme disease has been reported in 47 states.

Distemper

This is virtually an incurable disease. If the dog recovers, he is subject to severe nervous disorders. The virus attacks every tissue in the body and resembles a bad cold with a fever. It can cause a runny nose and eyes and cause gastrointestinal disorders, including a poor appetite, vomiting and diarrhea. The virus is carried by raccoons, foxes, wolves, mink and other dogs. Unvaccinated youngsters and senior citizens are very susceptible. This is still a common disease.

Hepatitis

This is a virus that is most serious in very young dogs. It is spread by contact with an infected animal or its stool or urine. The virus affects the liver and kidneys and is characterized by high fever, depression and lack of appetite. Recovered animals may be afflicted with chronic illnesses.

It is especially important for puppies to be vaccinated if they are kept with other puppies or if they will be spending time around other dogs.

Leptospirosis

This is a bacterial disease transmitted by contact with the urine of an infected dog, rat or other wildlife. It produces severe symptoms of fever, depression, jaundice and internal bleeding and was fatal before the vaccine was developed. Recovered dogs can be carriers, and the disease can be transmitted from dogs to humans.

Bordetella attached to canine cilia. Otherwise known as kennel cough, this disease is highly contagious and should be vaccinated against routinely.

Parvovirus

This was first noted in the late 1970s and is still a fatal disease. However, with proper vaccinations, early diagnosis and prompt treatment, it is a manageable disease. It attacks the bone marrow and intestinal tract. The symptoms include depression, loss of appetite, vomiting, diarrhea and collapse. Immediate medical attention is of the essence.

Rabies

This is shed in the saliva and is carried by raccoons, skunks, foxes, other dogs and cats. It attacks nerve tissue, resulting in paralysis and death. Rabies can be transmitted to people and is virtually always fatal. This disease is reappearing in the suburbs.

Bordetella (Kennel Cough)

The symptoms are coughing, sneezing, hacking and retching accompanied by nasal discharge usually lasting from a few days to several weeks. There are several disease-producing organisms responsible for this disease. The present vaccines are helpful but do not protect for all the strains. It usually is not life threatening but in some instances it can progress to a serious bronchopneumonia. The disease is highly contagious. The vaccination should be given routinely for dogs that come in contact with other dogs, such as through boarding, training class or visits to the groomer.

Coronavirus

This is usually self limiting and not life threatening. It was first noted in the late '70s about a year before parvovirus. The virus produces a yellow/brown stool and there may be depression, vomiting and diarrhea.

Lyme Disease

This was first diagnosed in the United States in 1976 in Lyme, CT in people who lived in close proximity to the deer tick. Symptoms may include acute lameness, fever, swelling of joints and loss of appetite. Your veterinarian can advise you if you live in an endemic area.

After your puppy has completed his puppy vaccinations, you will continue to booster the DHLPP once a year. It is customary to booster the rabies one year after the first vaccine and then, depending on where you live, it should be boostered every year or every three years. This depends on your local laws. The Lyme and corona vaccines are boostered annually and it is recommended that the bordetella be boostered every six to eight months.

ANNUAL VISIT

I would like to impress the importance of the annual check up, which would include the booster vaccinations, check for intestinal parasites and test for heartworm. Today in our very busy world it is rush, rush and see "how much you can get for how little." Unbelievably, some non-veterinary businesses have entered into the vaccination business. More harm than good can come to your dog through improper vaccinations, possibly

Laboratory tests are studied by highly trained veterinary technicians. Most tests are performed right in the veterinarian's office, and results are usually ready on the same day.

from inferior vaccines and/or the wrong schedule. More than likely you truly care about your companion dog and over the years you have devoted much time and expense to his well being. Perhaps you are unaware that a vaccination is not just a vaccination. There is more involved. Please, please follow through with regular physical examinations. It is so important for your veterinarian to know your dog and this is especially true during middle age through the geriatric years. More than likely your older dog will require more than one physical a

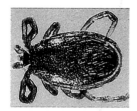

The deer tick is the most common carrier of Lyme disease. Photo courtesy of Virbac Laboratories, Inc., Fort Worth, Texas.

Keep your APBT healthy and playful with regular visits to the veterinarian.

year. The annual physical is good preventive medicine. Through early diagnosis and subsequent treatment your dog can maintain a longer and better quality of life.

INTESTINAL PARASITES

Hookworms

These are almost microscopic intestinal worms that can cause anemia and therefore serious problems, including death, in young puppies. Hookworms can be transmitted to humans through penetration of the skin. Puppies may be born with them.

Roundworms

These are spaghetti-like worms that can cause a potbellied appearance and dull coat along with more severe symptoms, such as vomiting, diarrhea and coughing. Puppies acquire these while in the mother's uterus and through lactation. Both hookworms and roundworms may be acquired through ingestion.

Whipworms

These have a three-month life cycle and are not acquired through the dam. They cause intermittent diarrhea usually with mucus. Whipworms are possibly the most difficult worm to eradicate. Their eggs are very resistant to most environmental factors and can last for years until the proper conditions enable them to mature. Whipworms are seldom seen in the stool.

Intestinal parasites are more prevalent in some areas than others. Climate, soil and contamination are big factors contributing to the incidence of intestinal parasites. Eggs are passed in the stool, lay on the ground and then become infective in a certain number of days. Each of the above worms has a different life cycle. Your best chance of becoming and remaining worm-free is to always pooper-scoop your yard. A fenced-in yard keeps stray dogs out, which is certainly helpful.

I would recommend having a fecal examination on your dog twice a year or more often if there is a problem. If your dog has a positive fecal sample, then he will be given the appropriate medication and you will be asked to bring back another stool sample in a certain period of time (depending on the type of worm) and then be rewormed. This process goes on until he has at least two negative samples. The different types of worms require different medications. You will be wasting your money and doing your dog an injustice by buying over-the-counter medication without first consulting your veterinarian.

OTHER INTERNAL PARASITES

Coccidiosis and Giardiasis

These protozoal infections usually affect puppies, especially in places where large numbers of puppies are brought together. Older dogs may harbor these infections but do not show signs unless they are stressed. Symptoms include diarrhea, weight loss and lack of appetite. These infections are not always apparent in the fecal examination.

Whipworms are hard to find unless one strains the feces, and this is best left to a veterinarian. These are adult whipworms.

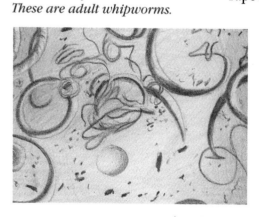

Tapeworms

Seldom apparent on fecal floatation, they are diagnosed frequently as rice-like segments around the dog's anus and the base of the tail. Tapeworms are long, flat and ribbon like, sometimes several feet in length, and made up of many segments about five-eighths of an inch long. The two most common types of tapeworms found in the dog are:

(1) First the larval form of the flea tapeworm parasite must mature in an intermediate host, the flea, before it can become infective. Your dog acquires this by ingesting the flea through licking and chewing.

(2) Rabbits, rodents and certain large game animals serve as intermediate hosts for other species of tapeworms. If your dog should eat one of these infected hosts, then he can acquire tapeworms.

HEARTWORM DISEASE

This is a worm that resides in the heart and adjacent blood vessels of the lung that produces microfilaria, which circulate in the bloodstream. It is possible for a dog to be infected with any number of worms from one to a hundred that can be 6 to 14 inches long. It is a life-threatening disease, expensive to treat and easily prevented. Depending on where you live, your veterinarian may recommend a preventive year-round and either an annual or semiannual blood test. The most common preventive is given once a month.

EXTERNAL PARASITES

Fleas

These pests are not only the dog's worst enemy but also enemy to the owner's pocketbook. Preventing is less expensive than treating, but regardless I think we'd prefer to spend our money elsewhere. I would guess that the majority of our dogs are allergic to the bite of a flea, and in many cases it only takes one flea bite. The protein in the flea's saliva is the culprit. Allergic dogs have a reaction, which usually results in a "hot spot." More than likely such a reaction will involve a trip to the veterinarian for treatment. Yes, prevention is less expensive. Fortunately today there are several good products available.

If there is a flea infestation, no one product is going to correct the problem. Not only will the dog require treatment

The cat flea is the most common flea of dogs. It starts feeding soon after it makes contact with the dog.

so will the environment. In general flea collars are not very effective although there is now available an "egg" collar that will kill the eggs on the dog. Dips are the most economical but they are messy. There are some effective shampoos and treatments available through pet shops and veterinarians. An oral tablet arrived on the American market in 1995 and was popular in Europe the previous year. It sterilizes the female flea but will not kill adult fleas. Therefore the tablet, which is given monthly, will

Dirofilaria—adult worms in the heart of a dog. It is possible for a dog to be infected with any number of worms that can be 6 to 14 inches long. Photo courtesy of Merck AgVet.

decrease the flea population but is not a "cure-all." Those dogs that suffer from flea-bite allergy will still be subjected to the bite of the flea. Another popular parasiticide is permethrin, which is applied to the back of the dog in one or two places depending on the dog's weight. This product works as a repellent causing the flea to get "hot feet" and jump off. Do not confuse this product with some of the organophosphates that are also applied to the dog's back.

Some products are not usable on young puppies. Treating fleas should be done under your veterinarian's guidance. Frequently it is necessary to combine products and the layman does not have the knowledge regarding possible toxicities. It is hard to believe but there are a few dogs that do have a natural resistance to fleas. Nevertheless it would be wise to treat all pets at the same time. Don't forget your cats. Cats just love to prowl the neighborhood and consequently return with unwanted guests.

Adult fleas live on the dog but their eggs drop off the dog into the environment. There they go through four larval stages before reaching adulthood, and thereby are able to jump back on the poor unsuspecting dog. The cycle resumes and takes between 21 to 28 days under ideal conditions. There are environmental products available that will kill both the adult fleas and the larvae.

Ticks

Ticks carry Rocky Mountain Spotted Fever, Lyme disease and can cause tick paralysis. They should be removed with tweezers, trying to pull out the head. The jaws carry disease. There is a tick preventive collar that does an excellent job. The ticks automatically back out on those dogs wearing collars.

Sarcoptic Mange

This is a mite that is difficult to find on skin scrapings. The pinnal reflex is a good indicator of this disease. Rub the ends of the pinna (ear) together and the dog will start scratching with his foot. Sarcoptes are highly contagious to other dogs and to humans although they do not live long on humans. They cause intense itching.

Demodectic Mange

This is a mite that is passed from the dam to her puppies. It affects youngsters age three to ten months. Diagnosis is confirmed by skin scraping. Small areas of alopecia around the eyes, lips and/or forelegs become visible. There is little itching unless there is a secondary bacterial infection. Some breeds are afflicted more than others.

Cheyletiella

This causes intense itching and is diagnosed by skin scraping. It lives in the outer layers of the skin of dogs, cats, rabbits and humans. Yellow-gray scales may be found on the back and the rump, top of the head and the nose.

TO BREED OR NOT TO BREED

More than likely your breeder has requested that you have

your puppy neutered or spayed. Your breeder's request is based on what is healthiest for your dog and what is most beneficial for your breed. Experienced and

Dogs that spend time outside, especially in grassy or wooded areas, need to be checked often for ticks.

Breeders sometimes sell puppies on the condition that the new owners have the puppies spayed or neutered. conscientious breeders devote many years into developing a bloodline. In order to do this, he makes every effort to plan each breeding in regard to conformation, temperament and health. This type of breeder does his best to perform the necessary testing (i.e., OFA, CERF, testing for inherited blood disorders, thyroid, etc.). Testing is expensive and sometimes very disheartening when a favorite dog doesn't pass his health tests. The health history pertains not only to the breeding stock but to the immediate ancestors. Reputable breeders do not want their offspring to be bred indiscriminately. Therefore you may be asked to neuter or spay your puppy. Of course there is always the exception, and your breeder may agree to let you breed your dog under his direct supervision. This is an important concept. More and more effort is being made to breed healthier dogs.

Spay/Neuter

There are numerous benefits of performing this surgery at six months of age. Unspayed females are subject to mammary and ovarian cancer. In order to prevent mammary cancer she must be spayed prior to her first heat cycle. Later in life, an

Having your puppy spayed or neutered at a young age will help lessen the puppy's risk of developing serious health problems later in life.

unspayed female may develop a pyometra (an infected uterus), which is definitely life threatening.

Spaying is performed under a general anesthetic and is easy on the young dog. As you might expect it is a little harder on the older dog, but that is no reason to deny her the surgery. The surgery removes the ovaries and uterus. It is important to remove all the ovarian tissue. If some is left behind, she could remain attractive to males. In order to view the ovaries, a reasonably long incision is necessary. An ovariohysterectomy is considered major surgery.

Neutering the male at a young age will inhibit some characteristic male behavior that owners frown upon. I have found my boys will not hike their legs and mark territory if they are neutered at six months of age. Also neutering at a young age has hormonal benefits, lessening the chance of hormonal aggressiveness.

Surgery involves removing the testicles but leaving the scrotum. If there should be a retained testicle, then he definitely needs to be neutered before the age of two or three years. Retained testicles can develop into cancer. Unneutered males are at risk for testicular cancer, perineal fistulas, perianal tumors and fistulas and prostatic disease.

Intact males and females are prone to housebreaking accidents. Females urinate frequently before, during and after heat cycles, and males tend to mark territory if there is a female in heat. Males may show the same behavior if there is a visiting dog or guests.

Surgery involves a sterile operating procedure equivalent to human surgery. The incision site is shaved, surgically scrubbed and draped. The veterinarian wears a sterile surgical gown, cap, mask and gloves. Anesthesia should be monitored by a registered technician. It is customary for the veterinarian to recommend a pre-anesthetic blood screening, looking for metabolic problems and a ECG rhythm strip to check for normal heart function. Today anesthetics are equal to human anesthetics, which enables your dog to walk out of the clinic the same day as surgery.

APBTs that receive proper health care throughout their lives will be able to provide you with companionship for many years.

Some folks worry about their dog gaining weight after being neutered or spayed. This is usually not the case. It is true that some dogs may be less active so they could develop a problem, but my own dogs are just as active as they were before surgery. I have a hard time keeping weight on them. However, if your dog should begin to gain, then you need to decrease his food and see to it that he gets a little more exercise.

DENTAL CARE for Your Dog's Life

So you've got a new puppy! You also have a new set of puppy teeth in your household. Anyone who has ever raised a puppy is abundantly aware of these new teeth. Your puppy will chew anything it can reach, chase your shoelaces, and play "tear the rag" with any piece of clothing it can find. When puppies are newly born, they have no teeth. At about four weeks of age, puppies of most breeds begin to develop their deciduous or baby teeth. They begin eating semi-solid food, fighting and biting with their litter mates, and learning discipline from their mother. As their new teeth come in, they inflict more pain on their mother's breasts, so her feeding sessions become less frequent and shorter. By six or eight weeks, the mother will start growling to warn her pups when they are fighting too roughly or hurting her as they nurse too much with their new teeth.

Not only is Nylafloss® a fun chew toy but it also aids in the proper development of a puppy's teeth.

Puppies need to chew. It is a necessary part of their physical and mental development. They develop muscles and necessary life skills as they drag objects around, fight over possession, and vocalize alerts and warnings. Puppies chew on things to explore their world. They are using their sense of taste to determine what is food and what is not. How else can they tell an electrical cord from a lizard? At about four months of age, most puppies begin shedding their baby teeth. Often these teeth need some help to come out and make way for the permanent teeth. The incisors (front teeth) will be replaced first. Then, the adult canine or fang teeth erupt. When the baby tooth is not shed before the permanent tooth comes in, veterinarians call it a retained deciduous tooth. This condition will often cause gum infections by trapping hair and debris between the permanent tooth and the retained baby tooth. Nylafloss® is an excellent device for puppies to use. They can toss

A thorough oral inspection should be a part of your dog's regular physical examination.

it, drag it, and chew on the many surfaces it presents. The baby teeth can catch in the nylon material, aiding in their removal. Puppies that have adequate chew toys will have less destructive behavior, develop more physically, and have less chance of retained deciduous teeth.

During the first year, your dog should be seen by your veterinarian at regular intervals. Your veterinarian will let you know when to bring in your puppy for vaccinations and parasite examinations. At each visit, your veterinarian should inspect the lips, teeth, and mouth as part of a complete physical examination. You should take some part in the maintenance of your dog's oral health. You should examine your dog's mouth weekly throughout his first year to make sure there are no sores, foreign objects, tooth problems, etc. If your dog drools excessively, shakes its head, or has bad breath, consult your veterinarian. By the time your dog is six months old, the permanent teeth are all in and plaque can start to accumulate on the tooth surfaces. This is when your dog needs to develop good dental-care habits to prevent calculus build-up on its teeth. Brushing is best. That is a fact that cannot be denied. However, some dogs do not like their teeth brushed regularly, or you may not be able to accomplish the task. In that case, you should consider a product that will help prevent plaque and calculus build-up.

The Plaque Attackers® and Galileo Bone® are other excellent choices for the first three years of a dog's life. Their shapes make them interesting for the dog. As the dog chews on them, the solid polyurethane massages the gums which improves the blood circulation to the periodontal tissues. Projections on the chew devices increase the surface and are in contact with the tooth for more efficient cleaning. The unique shape and consistency prevent your dog from exerting excessive force on his own teeth or from breaking off pieces of the bone. If your dog is an aggressive chewer or weighs more than 55 pounds (25 kg), you should consider giving him a Nylabone®, the most durable chew product on the market.

The Gumabone®, made by the Nylabone Company, is constructed of strong polyurethane, which is softer than nylon. Less powerful chewers prefer the Gumabones® to the Nylabones®. A super option for your dog is the Hercules Bone®, a uniquely shaped bone named after the great Olympian for its exceptional strength. Like all Nylabone products, they are specially scented to make them attractive to your dog. Ask your veterinarian about these bones and he will validate the good doctor's prescription: Nylabones® not only give your dog a good chewing workout but also help to save your dog's teeth (and even his life, as it protects him from possible fatal periodontal diseases).

By the time dogs are four years old, 75% of them have periodontal disease. It is the most common infection in dogs. Yearly

The softer composition of the Gumabone® was made especially for puppies and less powerful chewers. This young APBT will eventually develop very strong teeth.

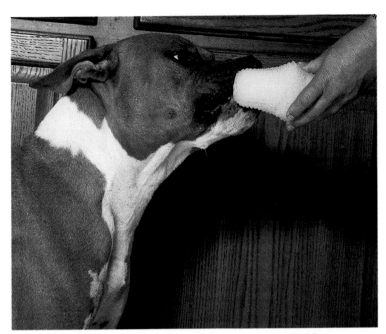

Plaque Attackers® are made in various shapes to make them interesting to dogs. The raised dental tips massage the gums and help clean the teeth as the dog chews.

examinations by your veterinarian are essential to maintaining your dog's good health. If your veterinarian detects periodontal disease, he or she may recommend a prophylactic cleaning. To do a thorough cleaning, it will be necessary to put your dog under anesthesia. With modern gas anesthetics and monitoring equipment, the procedure is pretty safe. Your veterinarian will scale the teeth with an ultrasound scaler or hand instrument. This removes the calculus from the teeth. If there are calculus deposits below the gum line, the veterinarian will plane the roots to make them smooth. After all of the calculus has been removed, the teeth are polished with pumice in a polishing cup. If any medical or surgical treatment is needed, it is done at this time. The final step would be fluoride treatment and your follow-up treatment at home. If the periodontal disease is advanced, the veterinarian may prescribe a medicated mouth rinse or antibiotics for use at home. Make sure your dog has safe, clean and attractive chew toys and treats. Chooz® treats are another way of using a consumable treat to help keep your dog's teeth clean.

Rawhide is the most popular of all materials for a dog to chew. This has never been good news to dog owners, because rawhide is inherently very dangerous for dogs. Thousands of dogs have died from rawhide, having swallowed the hide after it has become soft and mushy, only to cause stomach and intestinal blockage. A new rawhide product on the market has finally solved the problem of rawhide: molded Roar-Hide® from Nylabone. These are composed of processed, cut up, and melted American rawhide injected into your dog's favorite shape: a dog bone. These dog-safe devices smell and taste like rawhide but don't break up. The ridges on the bones help to fight tartar build-up on the teeth and they last ten times longer than the usual rawhide chews.

Nylabone® products are made to be especially appealing to dogs. This APBT pup enjoys a chicken-flavored Nylabone® and helps keep his teeth healthy at the same time.

As your dog ages, professional examination and cleaning should become more frequent. The mouth

Give your APBT good dental care throughout his life and he will always be able to flash a healthy smile!

should be inspected at least once a year. Your veterinarian may recommend visits every six months. In the geriatric patient, organs such as the heart, liver, and kidneys do not function as well as when they were young. Your veterinarian will probably want to test these organs' functions prior to using general anesthesia for dental cleaning. If your dog is a good chewer and you work closely with your veterinarian, your dog can keep all of its teeth all of its life. However, as your dog ages, his sense of smell, sight, and taste will diminish. He may not have the desire to chase, trap or chew his toys. He will also not have the energy to chew for long periods, as arthritis and periodontal disease make chewing painful. This will leave you with more responsibility for keeping his teeth clean and healthy. The dog that would not let you brush his teeth at one year of age, may let you brush his teeth now that he is ten years old.

If you train your dog with good chewing habits as a puppy, he will have healthier teeth throughout his life.

IDENTIFICATION and Finding the Lost Dog

There are several ways of identifying your dog. The old standby is a collar with dog license, rabies, and ID tags. Unfortunately collars have a way of being separated from the dog and tags fall off. I am not suggesting you shouldn't use a collar and tags. If they stay intact and on the dog, they are the quickest way of identification.

For several years owners have been tattooing their dogs. Some tattoos use a number with a registry. Here lies the problem because there are several registries to check. If you wish to tattoo, use your social security number. The humane shelters have the means to trace it. It is usually done on the inside of the rear thigh. The area is first shaved and numbed. There is no pain, although a few dogs do not like the buzzing sound. Occasionally tattooing is not legible and needs to be redone.

The newest method of identification is microchipping. The microchip is a computer chip that is no larger than a grain of rice. The veterinarian implants it by injection between the shoulder blades. The dog feels no discomfort. If your dog is lost and picked up by the humane society, they can trace you by scanning the microchip, which has its own code. Microchip

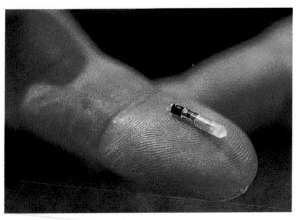

The newest method of identification is micro-chipping. The microchip is a computer chip that is no bigger than a grain of rice.

scanners are friendly to other brands of microchips and their registries. The microchip comes with a dog tag saying the dog is microchipped. It is the safest way of identifying your dog.

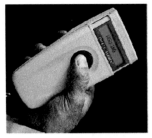

FINDING THE LOST DOG

I am sure you will agree with me that there would be little worse than losing your dog.

A fence can be helpful in keeping your dog in the yard, but be aware that a creative APBT can often find a way to escape.

The microchip code is picked up by a scanner, and the code traces the lost dog back to his owner.

Responsible pet owners rarely lose their dogs. They do not let their dogs run free because they don't want harm to come to

them. Not only that but in most, if not all, states there is a leash law.

Beware of fenced-in yards. They can be a hazard. Dogs find ways to escape either over or under the fence. Another fast exit is through the gate that perhaps the neighbor's child left unlocked.

Below is a list that hopefully will be of help to you if you need it. Remember don't give up, keep looking. Your dog is worth your efforts.

It is useful to have a good, clear photograph of your dog. The photo can be put on fliers and distributed if your dog is ever lost or missing.

1. Contact your neighbors and put flyers with a photo on it in their mailboxes. Information you should include would be the dog's name, breed, sex, color, age, source of identification, when your dog was last seen and where, and your name and phone numbers. It may be helpful to say the dog needs medical care. Offer a *reward*.

2. Check all local shelters daily. It is also possible for your dog to be picked up away from home and end up in an out-of-the-way shelter. Check these too. Go in person. It is not good enough to call. Most shelters are limited on the time they can hold dogs then they are put up for adoption or euthanized. There is the possibility that your dog will not make it to the shelter for several days. Your dog could have been wandering or someone may have tried to keep him.

3. Notify all local veterinarians. Call and send flyers.

4. Call your breeder. Frequently breeders are contacted when one of their breed is found.

5. Contact the rescue group for your breed.

6. Contact local schools—children may have seen your dog.

7. Post flyers at the schools, groceries, gas stations, convenience stores, veterinary clinics, groomers and any other place that will allow them.

8. Advertise in the newspaper.

9. Advertise on the radio.

TRAVELING with Your Dog

The earlier you start traveling with your new puppy or dog, the better. He needs to become accustomed to traveling. However, some dogs are nervous riders and become carsick easily. It is helpful if he starts with an empty stomach. Do not despair, as it will go better if you continue taking him with you on short fun rides. How would you feel if every time you rode in the car you stopped at the doctor's for an injection? You would soon dread that nasty car. Older dogs that tend to get carsick may have more of a problem adjusting to traveling. Those dogs that are having a serious problem may benefit from some medication prescribed by the veterinarian.

This APBT has become so accustomed to car travel that he looks right at home in the driver's seat!

Do give your dog a chance to relieve himself before getting into the car. It is a good idea to be prepared for a clean up with a leash, paper towels, bag and terry cloth towel.

The safest place for your dog is in a fiberglass crate, although close confinement can promote carsickness in some dogs. If your dog is nervous you can try letting him ride on the seat next to you or in someone's lap.

An alternative to the crate would be to use a car harness made for dogs and/or a safety strap attached to the harness or collar. Whatever you do, do not let your dog ride in the back of a pickup truck unless he is securely tied on a very short lead. I've seen trucks

Your new APBT pup may have never ridden in a car before. It is up to you to introduce him to car travel.

stop quickly and, even though the dog was tied, it fell out and was dragged.

I do occasionally let my dogs ride loose with me because I really enjoy their companionship, but in all honesty they are safer in their crates. I have a friend whose van rolled in an accident but his dogs, in their fiberglass crates, were not injured nor did they escape. Another advantage of the crate is that it is a safe place to leave him if you need to run into the store. Otherwise you wouldn't be able to leave the windows down. Keep in mind that while many dogs are overly protective in their crates, this may not be enough to deter dognappers. In some states it is against the law to leave a dog in the car unattended.

Never leave a dog loose in the car wearing a collar and leash. I have known more than one dog that has killed himself by hanging. Do not let him put his head out an open window. Foreign debris can be blown into his eyes. When leaving your dog unattended in a car, consider the temperature. It can take less than five minutes to reach temperatures over 100 degrees Fahrenheit.

TRIPS

Perhaps you are taking a trip. Give consideration to what is best for your dog—traveling with you or boarding. When

traveling by car, van or motor home, you need to think ahead about locking your vehicle. In all probability you have many valuables in the car and do not wish to leave it unlocked. Perhaps most valuable and not replaceable is your dog. Give thought to securing your vehicle and providing adequate ventilation for him. Another consideration for you when traveling with your dog is medical problems that

A car-seat harness is designed to protect dogs from injury by securing them in place and preventing them from disturbing drivers and passengers. Photo courtesy of Four Paws.

When traveling with your dog, you may want to bring along something familiar to make him feel more comfortable. This APBT isn't going anywhere without his water bowl!

may arise and little inconveniences, such as exposure to external parasites. Some areas of the country are quite flea infested. You may want to carry flea spray with you. This is even a good idea when staying in motels. Quite possibly you are not the only occupant of the room.

Unbelievably many motels and even hotels do allow canine guests, even some very first-class ones. Gaines Pet Foods Corporation publishes *Touring With Towser*, a directory of domestic hotels and motels that accommodate guests with dogs. Their address is Gaines TWT, PO Box 5700, Kankakee, IL, 60902. I would recommend you call ahead to any motel that you may be considering and see if they accept pets. Sometimes it is necessary to pay a deposit against room damage. Of course you are more likely to gain accommodations for a small dog than a large dog. Also the management feels reassured when you mention that your dog will be crated. Since my dogs tend to bark when I leave the room, I leave the TV on nearly full blast to deaden the noises outside that tend to encourage my dogs to bark. If you do travel with your dog, take along plenty of baggies so that you can clean up after him. When we all do our share in cleaning up, we make it possible for motels to continue accepting our pets. As a matter of fact, you should practice cleaning up everywhere you take your dog.

Depending on where your are traveling, you may need an up-to-date health certificate issued by your veterinarian. It is good policy to take along your dog's medical information, which would include the name, address and phone number of your veterinarian, vaccination record, rabies certificate, and any medication he is taking.

AIR TRAVEL

When traveling by air, you need to contact the airlines to check their policy. Usually you have to make arrangements up to a couple of weeks in advance for traveling with your dog. The airlines require your dog to travel

Many motels and airlines have certain policies and restrictions regarding traveling with pets. Make sure you investigate these before you bring your dog along.

Airlines require that pets travel in crates. The trip will be much easier on your APBT if he is already accustomed to spending time in a crate.

in an airline approved fiberglass crate. Usually these can be purchased through the airlines but they are also readily available in most pet-supply stores. If your dog is not accustomed to a crate, then it is a good idea to get him acclimated to it before your trip. The day of the actual trip you should withhold water about one hour ahead of departure and no food for about 12 hours. The airlines generally have temperature restrictions, which do not allow pets to travel if it is either too cold or too hot. Frequently these restrictions are based on the temperatures at the departure and arrival airports. It's best to inquire about a health certificate. These usually need to be issued within ten days of departure. You should arrange for non-stop, direct flights and if a commuter plane should be involved, check to see if it will carry dogs. Some don't. The Humane Society of the United States has put together a tip sheet for airline traveling. You can receive a copy by sending a self-addressed stamped envelope to:

The Humane Society of the United States
Tip Sheet
2100 L Street NW
Washington, DC 20037.

Regulations differ for traveling outside of the country and are sometimes changed without notice. Well in advance you need to write or call the appropriate consulate or agricultural department for instructions. Some countries have lengthy quarantines (six months), and countries differ in their rabies vaccination requirements. For instance, it may have to be given at least 30 days ahead of your departure.

Do make sure your dog is wearing proper identification. You never know when you might be in an accident and separated from your dog. Or your dog could be frightened and somehow manage to escape and run away. When I travel, my dogs wear collars with engraved nameplates with my name, phone number and city.

A reputable boarding kennel will require that dogs receive the vaccination for kennel cough no less than two weeks before their scheduled stay.

Another suggestion would be to carry in-case-of-emergency instructions. These would include the address and phone number of a relative or friend, your veterinarian's name, address and phone number, and your dog's medical information.

BOARDING KENNELS

Perhaps you have decided that you need to board your dog. Your veterinarian can recommend a good boarding facility or possibly a pet sitter that will come to your house. It is customary for the boarding kennel to ask for proof of vaccination for the DHLPP, rabies and bordetella vaccine. The bordetella should have been given within six months of boarding. This is for your protection. If they do not ask for this

Some dogs will get so used to traveling that they may actually like it! proof I would not board at their kennel. Ask about flea control. Those dogs that suffer flea-bite allergy can get in trouble at a boarding kennel. Unfortunately boarding kennels are limited on how much they are able to do.

For more information on pet sitting, contact NAPPS:
National Association of Professional Pet Sitters
1200 G Street, NW
Suite 760
Washington, DC 20005.

Our clinic has technicians that pet sit and technicians that board clinic patients in their homes. This may be an alternative for you. Ask your veterinarian if they have an employee that can help you. There is a definite advantage of having a technician care for your dog, especially if your dog is on medication or is a senior citizen.

You can write for a copy of *Traveling With Your Pet* from ASPCA, Education Department, 441 E. 92nd Street, New York, NY 10128.

BEHAVIOR and Canine Communication

Studies of the human/animal bond point out the importance of the unique relationships that exist between people and their pets. Those of us who share our lives with pets understand the special part they play through companionship, service and protection.

Senior citizens show more concern for their own eating habits when they have the responsibility of feeding a dog. Seeing that their dog is routinely exercised encourages the owner to think of schedules that otherwise may seem unimportant to the senior citizen. The older owner may be arthritic and feeling poorly but with responsibility for his dog he has a reason to get up and get moving. It is a big plus if his dog is an attention seeker who will demand such from his owner.

Over the last couple of decades, it has been shown that pets relieve the stress of those who lead busy lives. Owning a pet has been known to lessen the occurrence of heart attack and stroke.

Many single folks thrive on the companionship of a dog. Lifestyles are very different from a long time ago, and today more individuals seek the single life. However, they receive fulfillment from owning a dog.

One of the many benefits of owning a family pet is that its care and feeding helps to teach the children about responsibility.

Most likely the majority of our dogs live in family environments. The companionship they provide is well worth the effort involved. In my opinion, every child should have the opportunity to have a family dog. Dogs teach responsibility through understanding their care, feelings and even respecting their life cycles. Frequently those children who have not been exposed to dogs grow up afraid of dogs, which isn't good. Dogs

Children who are exposed to dogs learn to love, understand, and respect animals; children with no exposure to dogs are often fearful of them.

Many people thrive on the friendly and loyal companionship that dogs provide. Look at this APBT's tail wagging at the sight of his owner!

sense timidity and some will take advantage of the situation.

Today more dogs are serving as service dogs. Since the origination of the Seeing Eye dogs years ago, we now have trained hearing

dogs. Also dogs are trained to provide service for the handicapped and are able to perform many different tasks for their owners. Search and Rescue dogs, with their handlers, are sent throughout the world to assist in recovery of disaster victims. They are life savers.

Therapy dogs are very popular with nursing homes, and some hospitals even allow them to visit. The inhabitants truly look forward to their visits. I have taken a couple of my dogs visiting and left in tears when I saw the response of the patients. They wanted and were allowed to have my dogs in their beds to hold and love.

Nationally there is a Pet Awareness Week to educate students and others about the value and basic care of our pets. Many countries take an even greater interest in their pets than Americans do. In those countries the pets are allowed to accompany their

Mako is a fine example of a well-rounded APBT. He is a prize-winning conformation show dog as well as a registered therapy dog.

Though all dogs are individuals, members of the same breed often tend toward similar behavior. Unfortunately, one ill-tempered dog often affects the entire breed's reputation.

owners into restaurants and shops, etc. In the U.S. this freedom is only available to our service dogs. Even so we think very highly of the human/ animal bond.

CANINE BEHAVIOR

Canine behavior problems are the number-one reason for pet owners to dispose of their dogs, either through new homes, humane shelters or euthanasia. Unfortunately there are too many owners who are unwilling to devote the necessary time to properly train their dogs. On the other hand, there are those who not only are concerned about inherited health problems but are also aware of the dog's mental stability.

You may realize that a breed and his group relatives (i.e., sporting, hounds, etc.) show tendencies to behavioral characteristics. An experienced breeder can acquaint you with his breed's personality. Unfortunately many breeds are labeled with poor temperaments when actually the breed as a whole is not affected but only a small percentage of individuals within the breed.

If the breed in question is very popular, then of course there may be a higher number of unstable dogs. Do not label a breed good or bad. I know of absolutely awful-tempered dogs within one of our most popular, lovable breeds.

Inheritance and environment contribute to the dog's behavior. Some naïve people suggest inbreeding as the cause of bad temperaments. Inbreeding only results in poor behavior if the ancestors carry the trait. If there are excellent temperaments behind the dogs, then inbreeding will promote good temperaments in the offspring.

Did you ever consider that inbreeding is what sets the characteristics of a breed? A purebred dog is the end result of inbreeding. This does not spare the mixed-breed dog from the same problems. Mixed-breed dogs frequently are the offspring of purebred dogs.

If your APBT is left unsupervised during the day, a Gumabone® Frisbee® will help keep him occupied, and hopefully, out of trouble.*
The trademark Frisbee is used under license from Mattel, Inc., CA, USA.

When planning a breeding, I like to observe the potential stud and his offspring in the show ring. If I see unruly behavior, I try to look into it further. I want to know if it is genetic or environmental, due to the lack of training and socialization. A good breeder will avoid breeding mentally unsound dogs.

Not too many decades ago most of our dogs led a different lifestyle than what is prevalent today. Usually mom stayed home so the dog had human companionship and someone to discipline it if needed. Not much was expected from the dog. Today's mom works and everyone's life is at a much faster pace.

Some APBTs will sleep all day if left alone— be prepared to come home to an energetic, exuberant dog who is ready to play!

The dog may have to adjust to being a "weekend" dog. The family is gone all day during the week, and the dog is left to his own devices for entertainment. Some dogs sleep all day waiting for their family to come home and others become wigwam wreckers if given the opportunity. Crates do ensure the safety of the dog and the house. However, he could become a physically and emotionally cripple if he doesn't get enough exercise and attention. We still appreciate and want the companionship of our dogs although we expect more from them. In many cases we tend to forget dogs are just that–*dogs* not human beings.

I own several dogs who are left crated during the day but I do try to make time for them in the evenings and on the weekends. Also we try to do something together before I leave for work. Maybe it helps them to have the companionship of other dogs. They accept their crates as their personal "houses" and seem to be content with their routine and thrive on trying their best to please me.

SOCIALIZING AND TRAINING

Many prospective puppy buyers lack experience regarding the proper socialization and training needed to develop the type of pet we all desire. In the first 18 months, training does take some work. Trust me, it is easier to start proper training before there is a problem that needs to be corrected.

The initial work begins with the breeder. The breeder should start socializing the puppy at five to six weeks of age and cannot let up. Human socializing is critical up through 12 weeks of age and likewise important during the following months. The litter should be left together during the first few weeks but it is necessary to separate them by ten weeks of age. Leaving them together after that time will increase competition for litter dominance. If puppies are not socialized with people by 12 weeks of age, they will be timid in later life.

No matter where you acquire your APBT puppy, you should always find out about the puppy's previous upbringing and socialization.

The eight- to ten-week age period is a fearful time for puppies. They need to be handled very gently around children and adults. There should be no harsh discipline during this time. Starting at 14 weeks of age, the puppy begins the juvenile period, which ends when he reaches sexual maturity around six to 14 months of age. During the juvenile period he needs to be introduced to strangers (adults, children and other dogs) on the home property. At sexual maturity he will begin to bark at strangers and become more protective. Males start to lift their legs to urinate but if you desire you can inhibit this behavior by walking your boy on leash away from trees, shrubs, fences, etc.

Perhaps you are thinking about an older puppy. You need to inquire about the puppy's social experience. If he has lived in a kennel, he may have a hard time adjusting to people and environmental stimuli. Assuming he has had a good social upbringing, there are advantages to an older puppy.

Training includes puppy kindergarten and a minimum of one to two basic training classes. During these classes

Socializing your puppy includes taking him out to different places and introducing him to other people and animals.

you will learn how to dominate your youngster. This is especially important if you own a large breed of dog. It is somewhat harder, if not nearly impossible, for some owners to be the Alpha figure when their dog towers over them. You will be taught how to properly restrain your dog. This concept is important. Again it puts you in the Alpha position. All dogs need to be restrained many times during their lives. Believe it or not, some of our worst offenders are the eight-week-old puppies that are brought to our clinic. They need to be gently restrained for a nail trim but the way they carry on you would think we were killing them. In comparison, their vaccination is a "piece of cake." When we ask dogs to do something that is not agreeable to them, then their worst comes out. Life will be easier for your dog if you expose him at a young age to the necessities of life— proper behavior and restraint.

A well-socialized and well-adjusted APBT will be friendly toward strangers and will welcome being petted.

UNDERSTANDING THE DOG'S LANGUAGE

Most authorities agree that the dog is a descendent of the wolf. The dog and wolf have similar traits. For instance both are pack oriented and prefer not to be isolated for long periods of time. Another characteristic is that the dog, like the wolf, looks to the leader—Alpha—for direction. Both the wolf and the dog communicate through body language, not only within their pack but with outsiders.

Every pack has an Alpha figure. The dog looks to you, or should look to you, to be that leader. If your dog doesn't receive the proper training and guidance, he very well may replace you as Alpha. This would be a serious problem and is certainly a disservice to your dog.

Eye contact is one way the Alpha wolf keeps order within his pack. You are Alpha so you must establish eye contact with

This APBT's body language is loud and clear—"Rub my belly!"

your puppy. Obviously your puppy will have to look at you. Practice eye contact even if you need to hold his head for five to ten seconds at a time. You can give him a treat as a reward. Make sure your eye contact is gentle and not threatening. Later, if he has been naughty, it is permissible to give him a long, penetrating look. I caution you there are some older dogs that never learned eye contact as puppies and cannot accept eye contact. You should avoid eye contact with these dogs since they feel threatened and will retaliate as such.

Body Language

The play bow, when the forequarters are down and the hindquarters are elevated, is an invitation to play. Puppies play fight, which helps them learn the acceptable limits of biting. This is necessary for later in their lives. Nevertheless, an owner may be falsely reassured by the playful nature of his dog's aggression. Playful aggression toward another dog or human may be an indication of serious aggression in the future.

Owners should never play fight or play tug-of-war with any dog
that is inclined to be dominant.

Signs of submission are:
1. Avoids eye contact.
2. Active submission—the dog crouches down, ears back
and the tail is lowered.
3. Passive submission—the dog rolls on his side with his
hindlegs in the air and frequently urinates.

Signs of dominance are:
1. Makes eye contact.
2. Stands with ears up, tail up and the hair raised on his
neck.
3. Shows dominance over another dog by standing at
right angles over it.

Typically, the larger, taller dog would be dominant to the small puppy, but this APBT puppy doesn't look like he's willing to share his Gumabone®.

Dominant dogs tend to
behave in characteristic
ways such as:

1. The dog may
be unwilling to
move from his
place (i.e.,
reluctant to give up
the sofa if the
owner wants to sit
there).
2. He may not
part with toys or
objects in his
mouth and may
show possessiveness with his food bowl.
3. He may not respond quickly to commands.
4. He may be disagreeable for grooming and dislikes to be
petted.

Dogs are popular because of their sociable nature. Those
that have contact with humans during the first 12 weeks of life
regard them as a member of their own species—their pack. All
dogs have the potential for both dominant and submissive
behavior. Only through experience and training do they learn
to whom it is appropriate to show which behavior. Not all
dogs are concerned with dominance but owners need to be
aware of that potential. It is wise for the owner to establish his

Dogs are sociable by nature. Here, Bonehead "socializes" with the owner of the local Italian water ice shop and gets a treat (and an orange tongue!).

dominance early on.

A human can express dominance or submission toward a dog in the following ways:

1. Meeting the dog's gaze signals dominance. Averting the gaze signals submission. If the dog growls or threatens, averting the gaze is the first avoiding action to take—it may prevent attack. It is important to establish eye contact in the puppy. The older dog that has not been exposed to eye contact may see it as a threat and will not be willing to submit.

2. Being taller than the dog signals dominance; being lower signals submission. This is why, when attempting to make friends with a strange dog or catch the runaway, one should kneel down to his level. Some owners see their dogs become dominant when allowed on the furniture or on the bed. Then he is at the owner's level.

3. An owner can gain dominance by ignoring all the dog's social initiatives. The owner pays attention to the dog only

when he obeys a command.

No dog should be allowed to achieve dominant status over any adult or child. Ways of preventing are as follows:

1. Handle the puppy gently, especially during the three- to four-month period.

2. Let the children and adults handfeed him and teach him to take food without lunging or grabbing.

3. Do not allow him to chase children or joggers.

4. Do not allow him to jump on people or mount their legs. Even females may be inclined to mount. It is not only a male habit.

5. Do not allow him to growl for any reason.

Puppies are living, breathing animals and should not be treated like toys. If a child handles a puppy with care and respect, the child will, in turn, gain the respect of the puppy.

6. Don't participate in wrestling or tug-of-war games.

7. Don't physically punish puppies for aggressive behavior. Restrain him from repeating the infraction and teach an alternative behavior. Dogs should earn everything they receive from their owners. This would include sitting to receive petting or treats, sitting before going out the door and sitting to receive the collar and leash. These types of exercises reinforce the owner's dominance.

Young children should never be left alone with a dog. It is important that children learn some basic obedience commands so they have some control over the dog. They will gain the respect of their dog.

FEAR

One of the most common problems dogs experience is being fearful. Some dogs are more afraid than others. On the lesser side, which is sometimes humorous to watch, my dog can be afraid of a strange object. He acts silly when something is out of place in the house. I call his problem perceptive intelligence. He realizes the abnormal within his known environment. He does not react the same way in strange environments since he does not know what is normal.

On the more serious side is a fear of people. This can result in backing off, seeking his own space and saying "leave me

alone" or it can result in an aggressive behavior that may lead to challenging the person. Respect that the dog wants to be left alone and give him time to come forward. If you approach the cornered dog, he may resort to snapping. If you leave him alone, he may decide to come forward, which should be rewarded with a treat. Years ago we had a dog that behaved in this manner. We coaxed people to stop by the house and make friends with our fearful dog. She learned to take the treats and after weeks of work she overcame her suspicions and made friends more readily.

Some dogs may initially be too fearful to take treats. In these cases it is helpful to make sure the dog hasn't eaten for about 24 hours. Being a little hungry encourages him to accept the treats, especially if they are of the "gourmet" variety. I have a dog that worries about strangers since people seldom stop by my house. Over the years she has learned a cue and jumps up quickly to visit anyone sitting on the sofa. She learned by herself that all guests on the sofa were to be trusted friends. I think she felt more comfortable with them being at her level, rather than towering over her.

Dogs can be afraid of numerous things, including loud noises and thunderstorms. Invariably the owner rewards (by comforting) the dog when it shows signs of fearfulness. I had a terrible problem with my favorite dog in the Utility obedience class. Not only was he intimidated in the class but he was afraid of noise and afraid of displeasing me. Frequently he would knock down the bar jump, which clattered dreadfully. I gave him credit because he continued to try to clear it, although he was terribly scared. I finally learned to "reward" him every time he knocked down the jump. I would jump up and down, clap my hands and tell him how great he was. My psychology worked, he relaxed and eventually cleared the jump with ease. When your dog is frightened, direct his attention to something else and act happy. Don't dwell on his fright.

Aggression

Some different types of aggression are: predatory, defensive, dominance, possessive, protective, fear induced, noise provoked, "rage" syndrome (unprovoked aggression), maternal and aggression directed toward other dogs. Aggression is the most common behavioral problem encountered. Protective breeds are expected to be more aggressive than others but with the proper upbringing they can make very dependable companions. You need to be able to read your dog.

Many factors contribute to aggression including genetics and environment. An improper environment, which may include the living conditions, lack of social life, excessive punishment, being attacked or frightened by an aggressive dog, etc., can all influence a dog's behavior. Even spoiling him and giving too much praise may be detrimental. Isolation and the lack of human contact or exposure to frequent teasing by children or adults also can ruin a good dog.

Lack of direction, fear, or confusion lead to aggression in those dogs that are so inclined. Any obedience exercise, even the sit and down, can direct the dog and overcome fear and/or confusion. Every dog should learn these commands as a youngster,

A stable, even-tempered APBT is one that is neither fearful nor aggressive.

and there should be periodic reinforcement.

When a dog is showing signs of aggression, you should speak calmly (no screaming or hysterics) and firmly give a command that he understands, such as the sit. As soon as your dog obeys, you have assumed your dominant position. Aggression presents a problem because there may be danger to others. Sometimes it is an emotional issue. Owners may consciously or unconsciously encourage their dog's aggression.

This smiling APBT looks like he's waiting for someone to come and pet him!

Other owners show responsibility by accepting the problem and taking measures to keep it under control. The owner is responsible for his dog's actions, and it is not wise to take a chance on someone being bitten, especially a child. Euthanasia is the solution for some owners and in severe cases this may be the best choice. However, few dogs are that dangerous and very few are that much of a threat to their owners. If caution is exercised and professional help is gained early on, then I surmise most cases can be controlled.

Some authorities recommend feeding a lower protein (less than 20 percent) diet. They believe this can aid in reducing aggression. If the dog loses weight, then vegetable oil can be added. Veterinarians and behaviorists are having some success with pharmacology. In many cases treatment is possible and can improve the situation.

If you have done everything according to "the book" regarding training and socializing and are still having a behavior problem, don't procrastinate. It is important that the problem gets attention before it is out of hand. It is estimated that 20 percent of a veterinarian's time may be devoted to dealing with problems before they become so intolerable that the dog is separated from its home and owner. If your veterinarian isn't able to help, he should refer you to a behaviorist.

Unfortunately, many people who have seen and heard negative media portrayals of dogs referred to as "pit bulls" believe that all APBTs are vicious and aggressive.

PROBLEMS

Barking

This is a habit that shouldn't be encouraged. Over the years I've had new puppy owners call to say that their dog hasn't learned to bark. I assure them they are indeed fortunate but not to worry. Some owners desire their dog to bark so as to be a watchdog. In my experience, most dogs will bark when a stranger comes to the door.

The new puppy frequently barks or whines in the crate in his strange environment and the owner reinforces the puppy's bad behavior by going to him during the night. This is a no-no. I tell my new owners to smack the top of the crate and say "quiet" in a loud, firm voice. The puppies don't like to hear the loud noise of the crate being banged. If the barking is sleep-interrupting, then the owner should take crate and pup to the bedroom for a few days until the puppy becomes adjusted to his new environment. Otherwise ignore the barking during the night.

Barking can be an inherited problem or a bad habit learned through the environment. It takes dedication to stop the barking. Attention should be paid to the cause of the barking. Does the dog seek attention, does he need to go out, is it feeding time, is it occurring when he is left alone, is it a protective bark, etc.? Presently I have a ten-week-old puppy that is a real loud mouth, which I am sure is an inherited tendency. Both her mother and especially her grandmother are overzealous barkers but fortunately have mellowed with the

Excessive barking can be an annoyance, but dogs also use their bark to "verbally" communicate. What is your APBT trying to tell you?

years. My young puppy is corrected with a firm "no" and gentle shaking and she is responding. When barking presents a problem for you, try to stop it as soon as it begins.

There are electronic collars available that are supposed to curb barking. Personally I have not had experience with them. There are some disadvantages to to the collar. If the dog is barking out of excitement, punishment is not the appropriate treatment. Presumably there is the chance the collar could be activated by other stimuli and thereby punish the dog when it is not barking. Should you decide to use one, then you should seek help from a person with experience with that type of collar. In my opinion I feel the root of the problem needs to be investigated and corrected.

Jumping up is usually the sign of a happy, affectionate dog, however, you must teach your APBT when this behavior is acceptable and when it is not.

In extreme circumstances (usually when there is a problem with the neighbors), some people have resorted to having their dogs debarked. I caution you that the dog continues to bark but usually only a squeaking sound is heard. Frequently the vocal cords grow back. Probably the biggest concern is that the dog can be left with scar tissue which can narrow the opening to the trachea.

Jumping Up

Personally, I am not thrilled when other dogs jump on me but I have hurt feelings if they don't! I do encourage my own dogs to jump on me, on command. Some do and some don't. In my opinion, a dog that jumps up is a happy dog. Nevertheless few guests appreciate dogs jumping on them. Clothes get footprinted and/or snagged.

I am a believer in allowing the puppy to jump up during his first few weeks. In my opinion if you correct him too soon and at the wrong age you may intimidate him. Consequently he could be timid around humans later in his life. However, there will come a time, probably around four months of age, that he needs to know when it is okay to jump and when he is to show off good manners by sitting instead.

Some authorities never allow jumping. If you are irritated by your dog jumping up on you, then you should discourage it from the beginning. A larger breed of dog can cause harm to a senior citizen. Some are quite fragile. It may not take much to cause a topple that could break a hip.

How do you correct the problem? All family members need to participate in teaching the puppy to sit as soon as he starts to jump up. The sit must be practiced every time he starts to jump up. Don't forget to praise him for his good behavior. If an older dog has acquired the habit, grasp his paws and squeeze tightly. Give a firm "No." He'll soon catch on. Remember the entire family must take part. Each time you allow him to jump up you go back a step in training.

Biting

All puppies bite and try to chew on your fingers, toes, arms, etc. This is the time to teach them to be gentle and not bite hard. Put your fingers in your puppy's mouth and if he bites too hard then say "easy" and let him know he's hurting you. I squeal and act like I have been seriously hurt. If the puppy plays too rough and doesn't respond to your corrections, then he needs "Time Out" in his crate. You should be particularly careful with young children and puppies who still have their deciduous (baby) teeth. Those teeth are like needles and can leave little scars on youngsters. My adult daughter still has a small scar on her face from when she teased an eight-week-old puppy as an eight-year-old.

Jumping up may be fine during playtime, but you will probably want to discourage your APBT from jumping on your guests.

Biting in the more mature dog is something that should be prevented at all costs. Should it occur I would quickly let him know in no uncertain terms that biting will not be tolerated. When biting is directed toward another dog (dog fight), don't get in the middle of it. On more than one occasion I have had to separate a couple of my dogs and usually was in the middle of that one last lunge by the offender. Some authorities recommend breaking up a fight by elevating the hind legs. This would only be possible if there was a person for each dog. Obviously it would be hard to fight with the hind legs off the

Handling your APBT requires mutual confidence and trust. A well-trained and well-socialized dog never considers biting his master.

Teach your APBT puppy correct behavior at an early age—he should always act as sweet as he looks!

ground. A dog bite is serious and should be given attention. Wash the bite with soap and water and contact your doctor. It is important to know the status of the offender's rabies vaccination.

I have several dogs that are sensitive to having mats combed out of their coats and eventually they have had enough. They give fair warning by turning and acting like they would like to nip my offending fingers. However, one verbal warning from me says, "I'm sorry, don't you dare think about biting me and please let me carefully comb just a little bit more." I have owned a minimum of 30 dogs and raised many more puppies and have yet to have one of my dogs bite me except during that last lunge in the two or three dog fights I felt compelled to break up. My dogs wouldn't dare bite me. They know who is boss.

This is not always the case for other owners. I do not wish to frighten you but when biting occurs you should seek professional help at once. On the other hand you must not let your dog intimidate you and be so afraid of a bite that you can't discipline him. Professional help through your veterinarian, dog trainer and/or behaviorist can give you guidance.

Digging

Bored dogs release their frustrations through mischievous behavior such as digging. For the life of me I do not understand why people own dogs only to keep them outside. Dogs shouldn't be left unattended outside, even if they are in a fenced-in yard. Usually the dog is sent to "jail" (the backyard) because the owner can't tolerate him in the house. The culprit feels socially deprived and needs to be included in the owner's life. The owner has neglected the dog's training. The dog has not developed into the companion we desire. If you are one of these owners, then perhaps it is possible for you to change. Give him another chance. Some owners object to their dog's unkempt coat and doggy odor. See that he is groomed on a regular schedule and look into some training classes.

Submissive Urination

This is not a housebreaking problem. It can occur in all breeds and may be more prevalent in some breeds. Usually it occurs in puppies but occasionally it occurs in older dogs and may be in response to physical praise. Try verbal praise or ignoring your dog until after he has had a chance to relieve himself. Scolding will only make the problem worse. Many dogs outgrow this problem.

Coprophagia

Also know as stool eating, sometimes occurs without a cause. It may begin with boredom and then becomes a habit that is hard to break. Your best remedy is to keep the puppy on a leash and keep the yard picked up. Then he won't have an opportunity to get in trouble. I do not like to clean up accidents or "poop scoop" the yard in front of puppies. I'm suspicious that some puppies try to help and will clean up the stool before I have a chance. Your veterinarian can dispense a medication that is put on the dog's food that makes the stool taste bitter. Of course this will do little good if your dog cleans up after other dogs.

Your dog's safety depends on a good tie-out set up. Although APBTs are protective of their homes and less likely to run, it pays to invest in a reliable, good quality set up.

The Runaway

There is little excuse for a dog to run away since dogs should never be off leash except when supervised in the fenced-in yard.

I receive phone calls on a regular basis from prospective owners that want to purchase a female since a male is inclined to roam. It is true that an intact male is inclined to roam, which is one of the reasons a male should be neutered. However, females will roam also, especially if they are in heat. Regardless, these dogs should never be given this opportunity. A few years ago one of our clients elected euthanasia for her elderly dog that radiographically appeared to have an intestinal blockage. The veterinarian suggested it might be a corncob. She assured him that was not possible since they hadn't had any. Apparently he roamed and raided the neighbor's garbage and you guessed it—

he had a corncob blocking his intestines. Another dog raided the neighbor's garbage and died from toxins from the garbage.

To give the benefit of the doubt, perhaps your dog escapes or perhaps you are playing with your dog in the yard and he refuses to come when called. You now have a runaway. I have had this happen on a smaller scale in the house and have, even to my embarrassment, witnessed this in the obedience ring. Help! The first thing to remember is when you finally do catch your naughty dog, you must not discipline him. The reasoning behind this is that it is quite possible there could be a repeat performance, and it would be nice if the next time he would respond to your sweet command.

Always kneel down when trying to catch the runaway. Dogs are afraid of people standing over them. Also it would be helpful to have a treat or a favorite toy to help entice him to your side. After that initial runaway experience, start practicing the recall with your dog. You can let him drag a long line (clothesline) and randomly call him and then reel him in. Let him touch you first. Reaching for the dog can frighten him. Each time he comes you reward him with a treat and eventually he should get the idea that this is a nice experience. The long line prevents him from really getting out of hand. My dogs tend to come promptly within about 3 to 4 feet (out of reach) and then turn tail and run. It's "catch me if you can." At least with the long line you can step on it and stop him.

Food Guarding

If you see signs of your puppy guarding his food, then you should take immediate steps to correct the problem. It is not fair to your puppy to feed him in a busy environment where children or other pets may interfere with his eating. This can be the cause of food guarding. I always recommend that my puppies be fed in their crates where they do not feel threatened. Another advantage of this is that the puppy gets down to the business of eating and doesn't fool around. Perhaps you have seen possessiveness over the food bowl or his toys. Start by feeding him out of your hand and teach him that it is okay for you to remove his food bowl or toy and that you most assuredly will return it to him. If your dog is truly a bad actor and intimidates you, try keeping him on leash and perhaps sit next to him making happy talk. At feeding time make him work for his reward (his dinner) by doing some obedience command such as sit or down. Before your problem gets out of control you should get professional help. If he is out of control over toys, perhaps you should dispose of them or at least put them away when young children are around.

Mischief and Misbehavior

All puppies and even some adult dogs will get into mischief at some time in their lives. You should start by "puppy proofing" your house. Even so it is impossible to have a sterile environment. For instance, if you would be down to four walls and a floor your dog could still chew a hole in the wall. What do you do? Remember puppies should never be left unsupervised so let us go on to the trusted adult dog that has misbehaved. His behavior may be an attention getter. Dogs, and even children, are known to do mischief even though they know they will be punished.

Does this APBT pup have the face of a mischief maker?

Your puppy/dog will benefit from more attention and new direction. He may benefit from a training class or by reinforcing the obedience he has already learned. How about a daily walk? That could be a good outlet for your dog, time together and exercise for both of you.

Separation Anxiety

This occurs when dogs feel distress or apprehension when separated from their owners. One of the mistakes owners make is to set their dogs up for their departure. Some authorities recommend paying little attention to the pet for at least ten minutes before leaving and for the first ten minutes after you arrive home. The dog isn't cued to the fact you are leaving and if you keep it lowkey they learn to accept it as a normal everyday occurrence.

This adorable APBT puppy looks like she needs someone to play with!

Those dogs that are used to being crated usually accept your departure. Dogs that are anxious may have a serious problem and wreak havoc on the house within a few minutes after your departure. You can try to acclimate your dog to the separation by leaving for just a few minutes at a time, returning and rewarding him with a treat. Don't get too carried away. Plan on this process taking a long time. A behaviorist can set down a schedule for you. Those dogs that are insecure, such as ones obtained from a humane shelter or those that have changed homes, present more of a problem.

Punishment

A puppy should learn that correction is sometimes necessary and should not question your authority. An older dog that has never received correction may retaliate. In my opinion there will be a time for physical punishment but this does not mean hitting the dog. Do not use newspapers, fly swatters, etc. One type of correction, that is used by the mother dog when she corrects her

It is impossible to completely "puppy-proof" your home. Try to keep your APBT pup occupied with a Nylaring®, and maybe he'll forget about your new carpet!

puppies, is to take the puppy by the scruff and shake him *gently*. For the older, larger dog you can grab the scruff, one hand on each side of his neck, and lift his legs off the ground. This is effective since dogs feel intimidated when their feet are off the ground. Timing is of the utmost importance when punishment is necessary. Depending on the degree of fault, you might want to reinforce punishment by ignoring your dog for 15 to 20 minutes. Whatever you do, do not overdo corrections or they will lose value.

My most important advice to you is to be aware of your dog's actions. Even so, remember dogs are dogs and will behave as such even though we might like them to be perfect little people. You and your dog will become neurotic if you worry about every little indiscretion. When there is reason for concern—don't waste time. Seek guidance. Dogs are meant to be loved and enjoyed.

The more that people learn about the APBT, the more they will appreciate the breed for being the intelligent, versatile, and sociable dogs they are.

References:

Manual of Canine Behavior, Valerie O'Farrell, British Small Animal Veterinary Association.

Good Owners, Great Dogs, Brian Kilcommons, Warner Books.

SUGGESTED READING

PS-613
*This is The
American Pit Bull
Terrier
176 pages, 120 full
color photos.*

H-1024
*The Book of The
American Pit Bull
Terrier
352 pages, over 190
full color photos.*

TS-142
*The Truth About
The American Pit
Bull Terrier
320 pages, over 300
full color photos.*

TS-141
*Pit Bulls and Tenacious
Guard Dogs
320 pages, over
300 full color
photos.*

TS-235
*The Working Pit
Bull
230 pages, over
300 full color
photos.*

H-1063
*The World of The
American Pit Bull
Terrier
288 pages, nearly
100 full color photos.*

INDEX